Sponsored by the Ocean Carbon & Biogeochemstry Program
with support from the:
National Science Foundation
National Oceanic and Atmospheric Administration
National Aeronautics and Space Administration
U.S. Geological Survey

Ocean Carbon and Biogeochemistry Scoping Workshop on Terrestrial and Coastal Carbon Fluxes in the Gulf of Mexico, St. Petersburg, FL May 6-8, 2008

Open-File Report 2009-1070

U.S. Department of the Interior
U.S. Geological Survey

Ocean Carbon and Biogeochemistry Scoping Workshop on Terrestrial and Coastal Carbon Fluxes in the Gulf of Mexico, St. Petersburg, FL, May 6-8, 2008

By L.L. Robbins, P.G. Coble, T.D. Clayton, and W.-J. Cai

Sponsored by the Ocean Carbon & Biogeochemstry Program
with support from the:
National Science Foundation
National Oceanic and Atmospheric Administration
National Aeronautics and Space Administration
U.S. Geological Survey

Open-File Report 2009–1070

U.S. Department of the Interior
U.S. Geological Survey

U.S. Department of the Interior
KEN SALAZAR Secretary

U.S. Geological Survey
Suzette M. Kimball, Acting Director

U.S. Geological Survey, Reston, Virginia: 2009

For more information on the USGS—the Federal source for science about the Earth, its natural and living resources, natural hazards, and the environment—visit *http://www.usgs.gov* or call 1-888-ASK-USGS

For an overview of USGS information products, including maps, imagery, and publications,
visit *http://www.usgs.gov/pubprod*

To order this and other USGS information products, visit *http://store.usgs.gov*

This report summarizes the results of the Ocean Carbon and Biogeochemistry Scoping Workshop on Terrestrial and Coastal Carbon Fluxes in the Gulf of Mexico that was held in St. Petersburg, Florida, May 6-8, 2008. This event was jointly sponsored by the Ocean Carbon and Biogeochemistry Program (OCB) with support from the National Science Foundation (NSF), the National Oceanic and Atmospheric Administration (NOAA), the National Aeronautics and Space Administration (NASA), and the U.S. Geological Survey (USGS). Recommendations set forth in this document do not necessarily reflect the positions of the United States Government.

Suggested citation:

Robbins, L.L., Coble, P.G., Clayton, T.D., and Cai, W.-J., 2009, Ocean Carbon and Biogeochemistry Scoping Workshop on Terrestrial and Coastal Carbon Fluxes in the Gulf of Mexico, St. Petersburg, FL, May 6-8, 2008: U.S. Geological Survey Open-File Report 2009-1070, 46 p.
The persistent URL for this report is *http://pubs.usgs.gov/of/2009/1070/*

Contents

Figures

Abbreviations

AUV	autonomous underwater vehicle
CDOM	colored dissolved organic material
CRP	Conservation Reserve Program
DEM	digital elevation model
DIC	dissolved inorganic carbon
DIN	dissolved inorganic nitrogen
DOC	dissolved organic carbon
DOM	dissolved organic matter
ECoS	Eastern Continental Shelf
EPA	Environmental Protection Agency
ESRL	Earth System Research Laboratory
FSLE	Florida Shelf Lagrangian Experiment
GIS	geographic information system
GMx	Gulf of Mexico
GOMECC	Gulf of Mexico and East Coast Carbon Cruise
IASNFS	Intra-Americas Sea Ocean Nowcast/ Forecast System
LOICZ	Land-Ocean Interactions in the Coastal Zone
LTER	Long-Term Ecological Research
MMS	Minerals Management Service
MOC	marine organic carbon

NACP	North American Carbon Program
NASA	National Aeronautics and Space Administration
NDBC	National Data Buoy Center
NEON	National Ecological Observatory Network
NERRS	National Estuarine Research Reserve System
NOAA	National Oceanic and Atmospheric Administration
OCB	Ocean Carbon and Biogeochemistry
OCCC	Ocean Carbon and Climate Change
pCO_2	partial pressure of carbon dioxide
PIC	particulate inorganic carbon
POC	particulate organic carbon
SGD	submarine groundwater discharge
SLR	sea-level rise
SPARROW	SPAtially Referenced Regressions on Watershed Attributes
SSS	sea surface salinity
SST	sea surface temperature
SWAT	Soil and Water Assessment Tool
TEM	Terrestrial Ecosystem Model
USDA	U.S. Department of Agriculture
USGS	U.S. Geological Survey

Ocean Carbon and Biogeochemistry Scoping Workshop on Terrestrial and Coastal Carbon Fluxes in the Gulf of Mexico, St. Petersburg, FL, May 6-8, 2008

By L.L. Robbins[1], P.G. Coble[2], T.D. Clayton[3], and W.-J. Cai[4]

Executive Summary

Despite their relatively small surface area, ocean margins may have a significant impact on global biogeochemical cycles and, potentially, the global air-sea fluxes of carbon dioxide. Margins are characterized by intense geochemical and biological processing of carbon and other elements and exchange large amounts of matter and energy with the open ocean. The area-specific rates of productivity, biogeochemical cycling, and organic/inorganic matter sequestration are high in coastal margins, with as much as half of the global integrated new production occurring over the continental shelves and slopes (Walsh, 1991; Doney and Hood, 2002; Jahnke, in press). However, the current lack of knowledge and understanding of biogeochemical processes occurring at the ocean margins has left them largely ignored in most of the previous global assessments of the oceanic carbon cycle (Doney and Hood, 2002). A major source of North American and global uncertainty is the Gulf of Mexico, a large semi-enclosed subtropical basin bordered by the United States, Mexico, and Cuba. Like many of the marginal oceans worldwide, the Gulf of Mexico remains largely unsampled and poorly characterized in terms of its air-sea exchange of carbon dioxide and other carbon fluxes.

In May 2008, the **Ocean Carbon and Biogeochemistry Scoping Workshop on Terrestrial and Coastal Carbon Fluxes in the Gulf of Mexico** was held in St. Petersburg, FL, to address the information gaps of carbon fluxes associated with the Gulf of Mexico and to offer recommendations to guide future research. The meeting was attended by over 90 participants from over 50 U.S. and Mexican institutions and agencies. The Ocean Carbon and Biogeochemistry program (OCB; *http://www.us-ocb.org/*) sponsored this workshop with support from the National Science Foundation, the National Oceanic and Atmospheric Administration, the National Aeronautics and Space Administration, the U.S. Geological Survey, and the University of South Florida.

The goal of the workshop was to bring together researchers from multiple disciplines studying terrestrial, aquatic, and marine ecosystems to discuss the state of knowledge in carbon fluxes in the Gulf of Mexico, data gaps, and overarching questions in the Gulf of Mexico system. The discussions at the workshop were intended to stimulate integrated studies of marine and terrestrial biogeochemical cycles and associated ecosystems that will help to establish the role of the Gulf of Mexico in the carbon cycle and how it might evolve in the face of environmental change. The information derived from the plenary sessions, questions, and recommendations formulated by the participants will drive future research projects. Further discussion of carbon dynamics is needed to address scales of variability, the infrastructure required for study, and the modeling framework for cross-system integration.

[1]U.S. Geological Survey, St. Petersburg, FL

[2]University of South Florida College of Marine Science, St. Petersburg, FL

[3]Ironwood Editorial Services, St. Petersburg, FL

[4]University of Georgia Department of Marine Sciences, Athens, GA

During the workshop, participants discussed and provided a number of priorities and recommendations, including:

☐ An integrated, three-pronged approach to the study of Gulf of Mexico carbon fluxes, utilizing field observations, remote sensing, and coupled physical-biogeochemical modeling

☐ A formal data-mining effort to compile existing datasets and identify critical data gaps

☐ Continuity of data collection, in terms of both frequency and duration

☐ The selection of Gulf of Mexico study sites using existing classification schemes and study sites

☐ Numerical modeling to help plan effective field campaigns and interpret results

☐ Development of linked, nested models, using existing Gulf of Mexico models as a good starting point

☐ A forum devoted to collaborative assessment of existing data, model capabilities, and potential barriers to model linking or coupling

☐ Initial determination of appropriate temporal and spatial scales for field observations, and modeling efforts to constrain Gulf of Mexico carbon fluxes

☐ With respect to infrastructure:

- An integrated network of terrestrial and marine carbon monitoring stations that build on existing infrastructure, with augmentation of capabilities where needed

- Recurring process cruises in the Gulf of Mexico

- The development of improved algorithms for interpretation of satellite remote sensing products

- A Gulf of Mexico data management center to provide measurement, modeling, and remote sensing products

- A common communication effort that uses existing networks and outreach opportunities to involve stakeholders and decisionmakers

Participants recognized that the key to understanding the Gulf of Mexico system requires international collaboration with scientists from countries adjacent to the Gulf of Mexico. Improved collaboration across existing research community boundaries will be critical and should be encouraged by the funding agencies.

Introduction

Background

North America has a major influence on the global carbon cycle—a cycle that is now out of balance (King and others, 2007), contributing to both the warming of the Earth's atmosphere (IPCC, 2007) and the acidification of the Earth's oceans (Kleypas and others, 2006). The continent is currently a net source of carbon dioxide (CO_2) to the atmosphere. In 2003, 85% of North American emissions came from the United States, 9% from Canada, and 6% from Mexico. The continent's land sink is about one-third the magnitude of its fossil-fuel emissions, making the continent a net source of carbon to the atmosphere (King and others, 2007).

As the United States, Mexico, and other countries move toward actively managing the flow of carbon—CO_2 specifically—through terrestrial, oceanic, and atmospheric reservoirs, reducing uncertainties in estimates of past, current, and future carbon fluxes grows increasingly important. Coastal oceans in particular remain a large unknown, though the quantification of carbon fluxes in coastal oceans is important for understanding the global carbon cycle and for informing public discourse and decisionmaking (King and others, 2007).

Complicating such a quantification effort, coastal processes are complex and highly dynamic, with rapid changes and large variations across small distances (Chavez and others, 2007). Ocean margins are characterized by intense geochemical and biological processing of carbon and other elements, and exchange large amounts of matter and energy with the open ocean. Topographic features, tidal mixing, turbulent physical circulation, and freshwater inflow from rivers and groundwater all contribute to small-scale intricacies. Biological productivity is generally elevated relative to open ocean areas, and the proximity of bottom sediments and land introduces additional biogeochemical complexity. Area-specific rates of productivity, biogeochemical cycling, and organic/inorganic matter sequestration are high in coastal margins, with as much as half the global integrated new production occurring over continental shelves and slopes (Walsh, 1991; Doney and Hood, 2002; Jahnke, in press).

Most studies of these highly dynamic regions have been local to regional in scope, and few synthesis products and models have been designed with the special case of coastal oceans in mind. The lack of knowledge and understanding of biogeochemical processes occurring at ocean margins makes it difficult to assess their contributions to the global carbon cycle (Doney and Glover, 2005).

It is not clear whether coastal oceans tend to be a net source or sink of atmospheric CO_2. Numerous studies support the view that a significant fraction of current ocean uptake of anthropogenic CO_2 may occur in continental-margin waters in the East China Sea (Tsunogai and others, 1999; Wang and others, 2000), North Atlantic European shelves (Kempe and Pegler, 1991; Frankignoulle and Borges, 2001; Thomas and others, 2004), U.S. Middle Atlantic Bight (Boehme and others, 1998; DeGrandpre and others, 2002; Vlahos and others, 2002), and larger river plumes such as those of the Amazon (Ternon and others, 2000; Kortzinger, 2003) and Mississippi Rivers (Cai, 2003; Lohrenz and Cai, 2006). These findings, however, stand in contrast to prevailing arguments that continental shelves must be net heterotrophic (Smith and MacKenzie, 1987; Smith and Hollibaugh, 1993; Mackenzie and others, 1998). The latter view is supported by recent reports on several low-latitude shelf systems, including the U.S. southeastern shelf (Cai and others, 2003), South China Sea (Zhai and others, 2005), major upwelling areas (Lefèvre and others, 2002), and tropical coastal margins (Chavez and others, 2007). These contrasting and conflicting reports highlight the need for an integrated study of carbon fluxes and regulatory processes in continental-margin waters in order to better understand processes regulating fluxes and to constrain estimates of coastal margins' contributions to overall oceanic CO_2 uptake.

Large uncertainties remain for North American coastal margins. With the exception of one or two isolated time series, little is known about historical trends in the coastal oceans' air-sea fluxes or source-sink behaviors (Chavez and others, 2007).

One major source of North American and global uncertainty is the Gulf of Mexico (GMx), a large semi-enclosed, subtropical basin bordered by the United States, Mexico, and Cuba (fig. 1). Like many coastal oceans worldwide, the Gulf remains largely unsampled and poorly characterized in terms of its air-sea exchange of carbon dioxide (fig. 2) and fluxes of other carbon species. Limited data indicate that Gulf and Caribbean waters are, on the whole, a strong CO_2 source (fig. 3). A recent synthesis suggests that GMx air-sea CO_2 flux may dominate the net flux of the entire North American margin because of the Gulf's large size and strong signals. Northern Gulf waters appear to be a strong local CO_2 sink (Cai, 2003; Chavez and others, 2007).

Interest in the Gulf of Mexico as a targeted study site has grown steadily over the past few years. A U.S. Carbon Cycle Science Plan (Sarmiento and Wofsy, 1999) proposed two long-term research goals: first, understanding the Northern Hemisphere land (carbon) sink, and, second, understanding the ocean carbon sink (with priority for regions in North America). Carbon cycling in ocean margins constitutes a critical link between these two atmospheric CO_2 sinks, as is recognized by several recent workshops and meetings organized by the North American Carbon Program (NACP) and the Ocean Carbon and Biogeochemistry (OCB) Steering Committee.

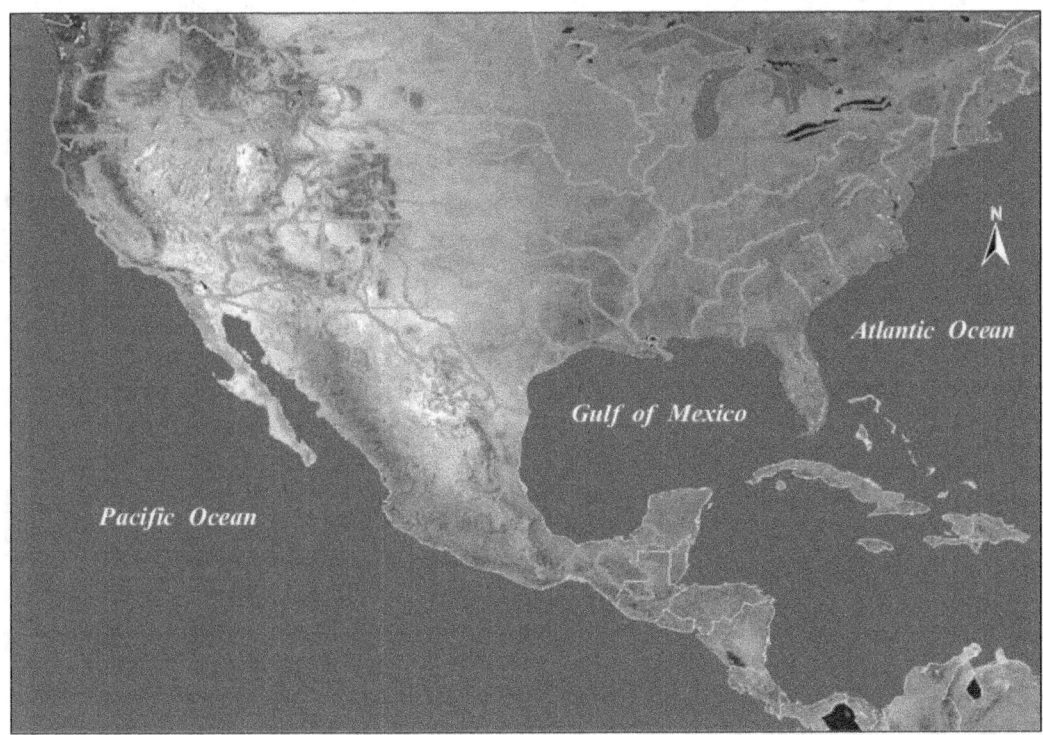

Figure 1. The Gulf of Mexico's surface drainage system covers more than 40% of Mexico and more than 60% of the United States.

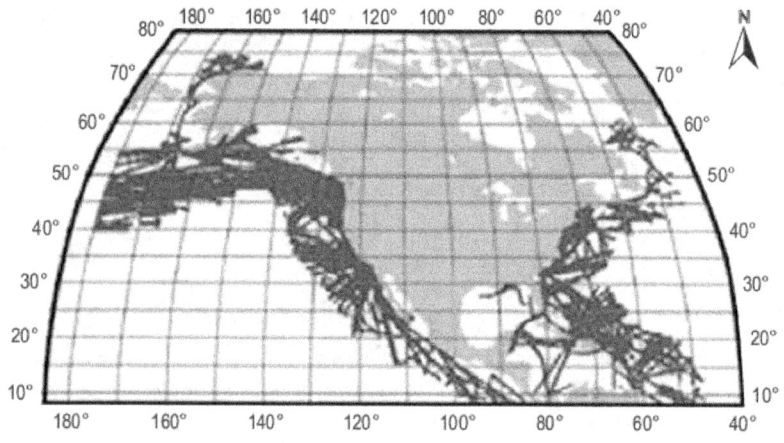

Figure 2. Distribution of coastal surface water CO_2 partial pressure measurements made between 1979 and 2004 (from Chavez and others, 2007).

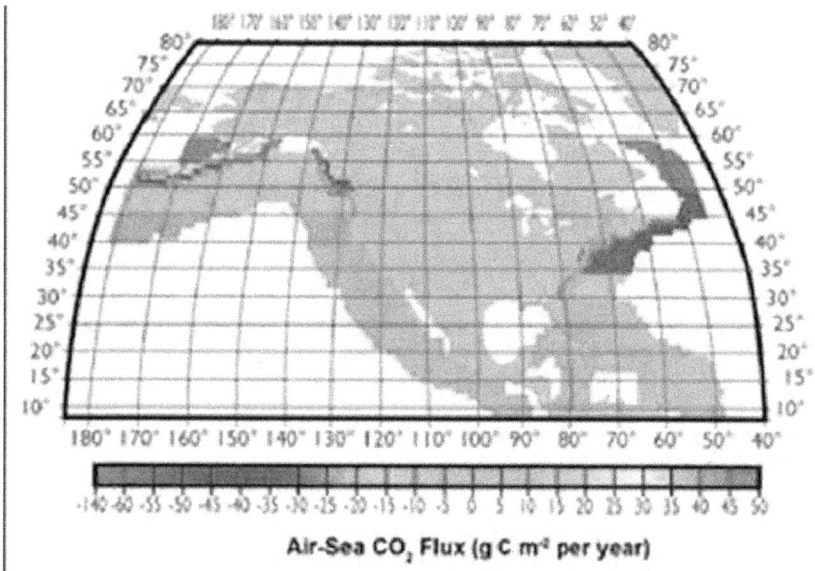

Air-Sea CO$_2$ Flux (g C m^{-2} per year)

Figure 3. Distribution of the annual mean air-sea net CO_2 flux over 1° x 1° pixel areas around North America. The green-yellow colors indicate that the ocean water is a source of CO_2; the magenta colors indicate a sink of atmospheric CO_2 (from Chavez and others, 2007).

A 2005 ocean carbon and climate change workshop, "The Ocean Carbon System: Recent Advances and Future Opportunities," highlighted the continental-margin carbon cycle as a key research area. Workshop participants noted that an improved understanding of coastal carbon processes will require a more extensive observational network (including field and remote sensing observations) across a diverse range of margin environments, such as river-dominated and upwelling regions (Doney and Glover, 2005).

Another 2005 meeting, "North American Continental Margins: A Synthesis and Planning Workshop," produced eight specific recommendations for improving knowledge of coastal carbon cycling (*http://www.whoi.edu/cms/files/ NACM_04.25_35943.pdf*). Participants noted the need for additional data, improved data synthesis, coastal models, remote-sensing algorithms, in-water technologies, and well-defined continental margin boundaries. Integrated process and synthesis studies were also recommended, with modeling

to proceed in parallel with (and not subsequent to) the in-water process studies. The need for field measurements to determine net fluxes of total carbon across key regime boundaries (for example, estuary-ocean, air-sea) was emphasized.

Terrestrial/coastal carbon fluxes and exchanges are also a priority of the newly formed OCB program. A 2007 OCB workshop breakout session identified several key questions to be considered in large-scale studies of coastal carbon processes. Of particular interest were an improved understanding of the intricacies of shelf processes (for example, lateral transport, denitrification, nitrogen fixation) and their implications for coastal carbon budgets—and, in turn, continental and global carbon fluxes. Climate change and resource management were also recognized as processes that impact watershed dynamics, coastal ecological processes, and biogeochemical cycles, including that of carbon (Benway and Doney, 2007).

The Gulf of Mexico provides an ideal venue for studying many of the key carbon issues identified in prior workshops and publications:

- The Gulf represents the single largest North American coastal-ocean source of atmospheric CO_2 (Chavez and others, 2007).

- The basin is semi-enclosed, facilitating the constraint of exchanges (Walsh and others, 1989).

- Including open water areas and coastal wetlands, the Gulf region covers more than 1.9 million square kilometers (km^2), with inflow from 33 major river systems (Yáñez-Arancibia and Day, 2004a).

- The Gulf's surface drainage system covers more than 60% of the United States and more than 40% of Mexico (Yáñez-Arancibia and Day, 2004b). The United States' Mississippi River [18,400 cubic meters per second (m^3/s) discharge (Benke and Cushing, 2005)] discharges directly onto the northern GMx shelf and represents one of the world's largest signals for carbon cycling. Mexico's Usumacinta-Grijalva rain forest river system [2,687 m^3/s (Benke and Cushing, 2005)] discharges directly onto the southern GMx shelf. The Gulf is also influenced by major river systems outside the Gulf proper, such as Venezuela's Orinoco River.

- In addition to rivers, the Gulf receives significant freshwater inflow from submarine groundwater discharge, especially along its eastern and southern margins. In some areas, groundwater discharge represents a significant influx of nutrients.

- The basin provides a variety of margin types—including wide carbonate shelves with significant groundwater inflow, a river-dominated muddy shelf, and a narrow upwelling shelf.

- The basin is subject to a wide variety of physical processes—including significant buoyancy inputs, major boundary current flow, upwelling, eddy intrusions, and frequent strong storms (including hurricanes).

- The Gulf is the site of significant nitrogen fixation, a process now recognized as important in carbon cycling and other aspects of ocean ecology and biogeochemistry.

- For the past two decades, the northern Gulf has been the site of persistent, widespread summer hypoxia (up to 20,000 km^2 in area), with significant ecological and economic impacts (Turner and others, 2005). Researchers expect the 2008 nitrogen-rich Mississippi River flood to produce the largest "dead zone" on record (Beeman, 2008).

- The Gulf of Mexico is significantly under-sampled in some respects. A recent compilation of North American coastal CO_2 measurements (Chavez and others, 2007; Hales and others, 2008) indicates a dearth of measurements in the region—to an extent rivaled only by the Gulf of California among all "lower 48" U.S. coastal waters.

- Due to its riverine and other connections to the North American continent, the Gulf represents a unique opportunity to study land/ocean interactions comprehensively.

In addition, a Gulf of Mexico carbon research program offers an excellent opportunity for international collaboration among agencies and scientists in the United States, Mexico, and Cuba.

Ocean Carbon and Biogeochemistry Scoping Workshop on Terrestrial and Coastal Carbon Fluxes in the Gulf of Mexico, St. Petersburg, FL, May 6-8, 2008

Workshop Motivation

Despite their relatively small surface area, ocean margins may have a significant impact on global biogeochemical cycles and, potentially, the global air-sea fluxes of CO_2. Margins are characterized by intense geochemical and biological processing of carbon and other elements and exchange large amounts of matter and energy with the open ocean. The area-specific rates of productivity, biogeochemical cycling, and organic/inorganic matter sequestration are high in coastal margins, with as much as half of the global integrated new production of carbon occurring over the continental shelves and slopes (Walsh, 1991; Doney and Hood, 2002; Jahnke, in press). However, the current gaps in knowledge and understanding of biogeochemical processes occurring at the ocean margins have left them largely excluded in most of the previous global assessments of the oceanic carbon cycle (Doney and Hood, 2002).

Contrasting reports that some margins are sinks of anthropogenic CO_2 and some are sources of CO_2 highlight the need for an integrated study of carbon fluxes and processes in continental margin waters in order to better understand processes regulating fluxes and better constrain the role of coastal margins' contribution to overall oceanic carbon cycling.

A U.S. Carbon Cycle Science Plan (Sarmiento and Wofsy, 1999) proposed two long-term research goals: first, understanding the Northern Hemisphere land (carbon) sink and second, understanding the ocean carbon sink (with priority for regions in North America). Understanding carbon cycling in ocean margins provides a critical link between these two atmospheric CO_2 sinks as is recognized by several recent workshops and meetings organized by the NACP and the OCB Steering Committee. A key area of uncertainty in current North American carbon budgets is the Gulf of Mexico. A recent synthesis (Chavez and others, 2007) suggests that the air-sea CO_2 flux from the Gulf of Mexico may dominate the net flux of the entire North American margins because of the large size and strong signals.

The Gulf of Mexico provides an excellent setting for large-scale study. Although it is a large body of water, its semi-enclosed nature makes it more feasible to constrain exchanges (Walsh and others, 1989). The Gulf of Mexico provides a wide variety of margin types (terrigenous clastic and carbonate sediments, narrow and broad shelves) and physical processes (buoyancy inputs, major boundary current, upwelling, eddy intrusions). The Mississippi River system represents one of the largest signals for carbon cycling in not just the North American continent but the entire world. A coordinated study in the Gulf of Mexico also provides an excellent opportunity for international collaboration with neighboring Mexico; scientists from this country have already expressed interest in such a study.

Workshop Goals

The Ocean Carbon and Biogeochemistry Steering Committee identified coastal carbon fluxes and exchanges as a priority topic for future research. At a recent Ocean Carbon and Biogeochemistry Workshop held in Woods Hole, MA, on July 23-26, 2007, a breakout group examined this topic and identified several key questions, including:

- Do continental margins represent a conduit for the large carbon signal that is currently unaccounted for in the terrestrial continental carbon budgets?

- What are the magnitudes and uncertainties of coastal carbon signals and to what extent will incorporation of more precise and accurate assessments of coastal carbon budgets into larger scale models improve the overall estimates of global carbon fluxes?

- How important are the intricacies of the shelf processes (lateral transport or cross shelf exchange, denitrification and nitrogen fixation, benthic processes, and ballasting of carbon and other elements by lithogenic materials) in regulating coastal carbon budgets?

- What are the impacts of climate change and resource management on watershed dynamics and coastal ecological processes, and what are the potential implications for biogeochemical cycles, including that of carbon?

This list is not exhaustive but identifies key issues that should be considered in large-scale studies of coastal carbon processes.

Workshop Description

The Ocean Carbon and Biogeochemistry Scoping Workshop on Terrestrial and Coastal Carbon Fluxes in the Gulf of Mexico was held in St. Petersburg, FL, on May 6-8, 2008. The goal of the workshop was to bring together researchers to discuss potential integrated research projects related to carbon fluxes and exchange in the Gulf. Approximately 90 scientists attended, representing U.S. and Mexican research organizations, academic institutions, and government agencies.

Twelve plenary speakers were asked to summarize the state of knowledge on carbon dynamics in various parts of the GMx system and to highlight processes of primary importance in controlling variability in fluxes and fates. During breakout sessions, conference participants were asked to build on the plenary information and formulate questions that will drive future research projects. Approximately 40 participants contributed posters.

The ultimate goal of future GMx research is to achieve an understanding of material and energy fluxes, exchanges, and fates so that we can anticipate river-ocean system changes related to global-scale climate changes. The workshop agenda, list of participants, background papers, and many of the presentations and posters are available online: *http://www.whoi.edu/sites/GMxCarbon/*

This document outlines the major findings and recommendations of this workshop. Special thanks are owed to all the hard-working discussion leaders and rapporteurs for excellent note-taking and write-ups of all the breakout sessions and especially for staying after the end of the conference to be sure their reports were completed. These include Barnali Dixon, Chris Anderson, David Butman, Kathy Tedesco, Bob Chen, Robyn Conmy, Ron Benner, Nazan Atilla, David John, John Paul, Miguel Goñi, Regina Easley, Simone Alin, Charles Perry, Lori Adornato, Liz Gordon, Carlos Del Castillo, and Laura Lorenzoni. Thanks also to the Steering Committee: Wei-Jun Cai, Scott Denning, Ben de Jong, Eileen Hoffman, Brent McKee, and Steve Lohrenz (ex officio). We are particularly grateful to all the participants for their engagement in discussions and valuable contributions to our knowledge base and recommendations for future research planning.

Overarching Research Question

Workshop participants developed the following overarching question to express the proposed general scope and orientation of a Gulf of Mexico carbon flux program:

What are the net fluxes of total carbon through the key interfaces defining the Gulf of Mexico system, how can future changes in these fluxes be predicted, and how will these changes impact ecosystems?

- □ The *Gulf of Mexico system* is here defined as including watersheds, margins, the open Gulf of Mexico, and the overlying atmosphere.

- □ *Key interfaces* of interest are land-atmosphere, soil-river, river-estuary, estuary-ocean, seafloor-water column, ocean-atmosphere, shelf-Gulf interior, and Gulf of Mexico-Atlantic.

- □ *Quantification of net fluxes of total carbon* (dissolved and particulate, organic and inorganic) is needed over sufficiently long time scales to represent irreversible transfers between reservoirs.

☐ Anticipated *future changes* include both natural and human-induced perturbations.

☐ Successful *prediction* of future changes will require process- and synthesis-level understanding of internal carbon cycling as well as the roles of relevant noncarbon elements (for example, nitrogen and phosphorus).

☐ *Ecosystem* refers to all physical and all biological components, including human, of the environment.

☐ Careful consideration of appropriate scales and resolution is required, and these may not be the same for prediction as for quantification of fluxes.

Key Recommendations

Key recommendations to answer the overarching research question provided by the workshop participants included:

☐ The study of the Gulf of Mexico as a whole system, from watersheds to open Gulf, rather than a conglomeration of parts.

☐ An integrated, three-pronged approach to the study of GMx carbon, utilizing field observations, remote sensing, and coupled physical-biogeochemical modeling.

☐ Comprehensive, cross-disciplinary data mining and model assessment, undertaken early in the program.

☐ Augmentation of existing programs to build a large-scale terrestrial and aquatic carbon-monitoring network and establish routine coastal process studies.

☐ Ongoing support for well-calibrated, long-term remotely sensed measurements and accompanying algorithm development.

☐ Interdisciplinary, multiscale modeling efforts that nest and link existing models, with emphasis on development of a community ocean circulation-biogeochemical model.

☐ Strategic investment in new technologies.

☐ Direct measurement of carbon and carbon-related fluxes across key interfaces (for example, air-sea CO_2 fluxes) will be required, along with accompanying process studies. Opportunities to maximize societal relevance, such as collaboration with economists and engagement in public outreach, should be encouraged.

☐ Long-term continuity of monitoring data is critically important. The elimination of stream gage and water quality monitoring stations and potential lapses in satellite ocean color measurements were cited as particular concerns.

☐ Facilitation of communication between GMx researchers, policymakers, stakeholders, and the general public must be a core program element. On this note, the community recommends:

- Support for international and interdisciplinary collaborations

- Development of a one-stop Web-accessible GMx data management center or enhancement of one of the many existing data management programs to include this focus

- Augmentation of existing communication networks and outreach opportunities to solicit public input and provide information about carbon cycle biogeochemistry and its social and economic implications

☐ Logistical support and assistance from the Ocean Carbon and Biogeochemistry program is desired in these specific areas:

- Administration of electronic lists to facilitate international, cross-disciplinary sharing of expertise and data among various subcommunities of researchers and stakeholders

- Mining of historical datasets

- Development and hosting of Web-based resources to receive and distribute information about GMx projects, research cruises, and so on

- Logistical support for field campaigns

- Data management, such as from GMx field campaigns

- Coordination of future meetings

Gulf of Mexico Carbon Fluxes: Knowns, Unknowns, and Uncertainties

Land-ocean interactions represent a major gap in our understanding of carbon fluxes and biogeochemical cycling. With its riverine and other connections to the North American continent, the Gulf of Mexico presents a special opportunity to study these interactions.

Gulf of Mexico Provinces: Priority Environments for Future Research

Among North American continental margins, the Gulf of Mexico (fig. 1) is distinctive in terms of its river-dominated shelves and strong episodic storm events. On the northern and southern margins, where rivers deliver large quantities of particulate and dissolved carbon, sediments, and nutrients, high rates of sediment deposition and primary productivity occur, along with episodic sediment resuspension and redistribution. On the eastern and western Gulf margins, the river imprint is relatively small, and Loop Current and upwelling processes predominate (Hales and others, 2008).

The Gulf is fed by more than 150 rivers, including 20 major river systems. The two largest are the Mississippi in the northern Gulf and the Usumacinta-Grijalva in the south. Freshwater inflow to the Gulf is approximately 10.6×10^{11} cubic meters per year (m^3/yr), with more than 64% of that total arriving via the Mississippi River. Other U.S. rivers contribute another 21%, and the remaining one-fifth is supplied from Mexico and Cuba (Nipper and others, 2004). South Texas receives the least rainfall among Gulf coastal areas, more than an order of magnitude less than the wet regions of the northern Gulf's Mississippi Delta and the southern Gulf's Tabasco Plain (Solis and Powell, 1999). Groundwater contributions are significant in many areas, especially the eastern and southern margins of the Gulf.

Thirty-nine major estuary systems rim the Gulf, 32 on the eastern and northern margins and 7 along the western and southern edges (Schroeder and Wiseman, 1999). Large marine-dominated bays occur in the east, river-dominated estuaries characterize the northern Gulf, and examples of coastal lagoons may be found in the south (Pennock and others, 1999). Most of the Gulf's estuaries are shallow [mean U.S. depth <2.5 m; (McKee and Baskaran, 1999)] and meteorologically dominated (Solis and Powell, 1999), with surface area and wind fetch higher than in other U.S. estuaries. Most are generally characterized by fine-grained sediments and frequent resuspension (McKee and Baskaran, 1999). Tidal influence on estuaries around the microtidal Gulf is relatively uniform (in contrast to freshwater influence), with tide ranges generally less than 1 m (Stumpf and Haines, 1998; McKee and Baskaran, 1999). The Mississippi River plume can be thought of as an unbounded estuary.

More than 14,500 km^2 of estuarine wetlands line Gulf coastlines. Approximately one third consists of forested mangrove wetlands, with the remainder being herbaceous marsh (Childers and others, 1998). Estuarine wetlands loss is a severe problem in all U.S. Gulf States (U.S. EPA, 1999), especially in the northern Gulf.

Human impacts, including eutrophication, are significant in some Gulf estuaries (Kennish, 2002). Nuisance and toxic algal blooms have been increasing in U.S. Gulf estuaries since the 1970s, and seagrass habitat has been declining. Fish biomarkers indicate fair to poor fish health in some areas of the northern Gulf, and shellfish bed closures have been significant (>25% of shellfish-growing waters) in most U.S. Gulf States (U.S. EPA, 1999).

Remote sensing coverage varies considerably over the basin. For ocean color measurements, satellite coverage, in terms of the percentage of clean pixels (Wanninkhof, 2008), is best over the carbonate shelves of the eastern and southern Gulf of Mexico (20-35% clean pixels) and poorest over the western basin.

The workshop participants recognized the Gulf of Mexico as five interconnected regions with distinctive physical forcings and biogeochemical characteristics and processes: the deep Gulf basin and four marginal regions (fig. 4). The central region (1) is a deep, semi-enclosed oligotrophic basin with an energetic circulation strongly connected to the Caribbean Sea and Atlantic Ocean. The eastern GMx shelf (2) is influenced by upwelling, river discharge, and a large but poorly quantified influx of groundwater. The northern GMx shelf (3) is river-dominated, receiving major discharge from the Mississippi-Atchafalaya River system. The narrow western GMx shelf (4) is dominated by upwelling and by eddies shed from the Loop Current. The southern GMx shelf (5) is influenced by upwelling and by groundwater and river (Usumacinta-Grijalva) discharge.

Open Gulf

The Gulf of Mexico (figs. 1, 4) is a dynamic, semi-enclosed subtropical/tropical sea. Of the total marine area, approximately 20% is continental slope and another 20% is abyssal plain. The average depth is about 1,600 m and the maximum depth is about 4,000 m (Nipper and others, 2004).

Because of its size and connectivity, the Gulf's contribution to global and regional processes is significant. The Gulf has a total marine area of about 1.5 million km^2 (Nipper and others, 2004), and its great volume implies that it has large gross (though perhaps not net) fluxes (such as nutrients, air-sea gas fluxes). The Gulf strongly participates in the North Atlantic gyre circulation, and recent studies indicate that circulation in the Gulf of Mexico and the Caribbean Sea are dynamically interdependent (Oey and others, 2005).

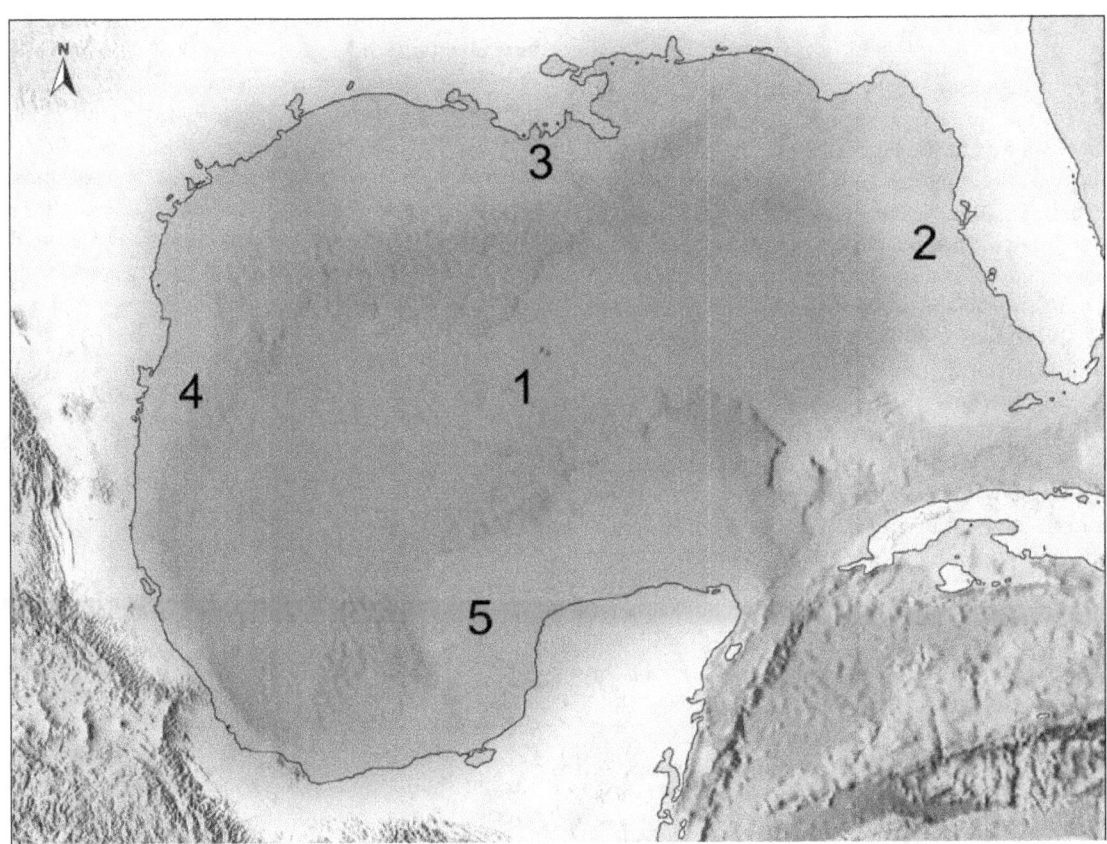

Figure 4. The Gulf of Mexico offers a variety of environments well suited for studying various aspects of carbon transport and related processes: (1) the open Gulf, (2) the West Florida shallow carbonate shelf, (3) the river-dominated northern shelf, (4) the narrow western shelf with its strong eddy-shelf interactions, and (5) the tropical Campeche Bay/Bank. Each region includes the watersheds of the streams and rivers that flow into the region's estuaries and onto the shelf.

The central basin region interfaces with each of the other GMx (margin) regions and is the integrator of all processes in all other regions. Studying only the shelf regions would yield an incomplete picture of carbon dynamics in the Gulf.

The Gulf of Mexico may be an important driver for fluxes of carbon from ocean to land. The North American Carbon Program is especially interested in the effect of Gulf air masses on the Mississippi River basin.

Dominant circulation features in the basin are the highly energetic Loop Current and its associated eddies (rings). Water enters the Gulf through the Yucatan Channel in the south, feeding the Yucatan/Loop western boundary current. The current then makes a wide, vigorous meander through the basin before flowing southward along the west Florida Shelf and exiting through the Florida Straits. The current and its rings (warm core rings in the western Gulf and cold core rings in the eastern Gulf) strongly interact with the basin's continental slope and shelves (Vukovich, 2007). As a result, the Loop Current drives many shelf processes.

Physical forcing in the Gulf is poorly parameterized. The broad range of spatial and temporal scales associated with GMx circulation contributes to the challenges the Gulf presents to numerical modelers (Oey and others, 2005), although there are many GMx circulation models in existence.

The Gulf of Mexico is a unique gas hydrate province (Milkov and Sassen, 2000). Natural gas hydrate, a mineral in which hydrocarbon and non-hydrocarbon gases are held within rigid ("icy") cages of water, typically occurs from depths of about 440 m to more than 2,400 m (Milkov and Sassen, 2000). These deposits represent an enormous potential reservoir of methane—and therefore a potential future energy resource and agent of climate change (Kvenvolden and Lorenson, 2007). The Gulf is unique in that both bacterial methane and thermogenic methane occur in shallow sediments and outcrops at the seafloor (Milkov and Sassen, 2000).

Eastern Gulf of Mexico

Terrestrial influences in the eastern Gulf (figs. 1, 4) arrive via local rivers, submarine springs, and aeolian dust. The southern two-thirds of the Florida peninsula is characterized by small rivers draining low-relief basins of less than 2,600 km^2 (Boning, 2008). To the north, two major rivers, the Suwannee and the Apalachicola, flow across the southeastern United States and into the Gulf. Their basins are characterized by moderate climate and abundant rainfall (Ward and others, 2005). Groundwater flows into the eastern Gulf from numerous freshwater springs on the West Florida Shelf (WFS), with concentrations of submerged springs found just off Tampa Bay and in the Aucilla River embayment (Hu and others, 2006). During summer months, aeolian (windborne) dust is supplied from Saharan West Africa to eastern Gulf and Caribbean waters, after a transit of thousands of kilometers across the Atlantic Ocean (Lenes and others, 2001).

Large marine-dominated bays are found along the eastern Gulf (Schroeder and Wiseman, 1999). Unlike most Gulf estuaries, these bays tend to show little intra-annual variability in salinity (Solis and Powell, 1999). Tides of the eastern Gulf margin are mixed but dominantly semidiurnal (Flick and others, 2003). Tidal range at Key West, FL, in the southeastern Gulf, is 0.56 m; at Cedar Key, FL, in the northeastern Gulf, it is 1.05 m. (Stumpf and Haines, 1998).

The land/sea boundary within this province is characterized by low-relief mangrove islands in the south, siliciclastic barrier islands in the central region, and marshes and limestone outcrops in the north. Episodic blooms, including headline-generating "red tides," have been observed on the eastern shelf, but for most of the year this system is oligotrophic (Hales and others, 2008). The seaward margin of the broad (100-150 km wide) carbonate shelf is defined by the precipitous 1,600-m drop-off of the Florida Escarpment (Sager, 2007).

The watersheds of the eastern Gulf have experienced explosive population growth over recent decades. Between 1990 and 2004, the Florida Gulf Coast population grew by 32.0%, from 4.07 million to 5.37 million; 2004-2006 brought another 4.6% growth. Population density during that period increased from 84 (1990) to 111 (2004) to 116 (2006) individuals/mi^2. The population growth rate was highest (56%, 1990-2003) in southwest Florida (Kildow, 2006, 2008).

The eastern Gulf is strongly influenced by the Loop Current and, seasonally, by Mississippi River outflow. The Loop Current occasionally intrudes upon the West Florida Shelf, generating a strong southward current of cold, nutrient-rich water along the shelf slope (He and Weisberg, 2003). When the Loop Current retreats (that is, does not intrude far into the Gulf), it can generate southward flow on the middle and inner shelf as well. Mississippi River waters interact with the shelf seasonally and after major flood events.

This region provides an interesting contrast with the northern Gulf of Mexico, in terms of riverine influences. Freshwater surface inflow in the eastern Gulf is much lower than in the northern Gulf. West Florida rivers differ from northern rivers in terms of not only discharge rates but also chemistry. For example, West Florida rivers typically have higher concentrations of dissolved organic matter (DOM) and can strongly influence optical properties and dissolved organic carbon (DOC) concentrations of shelf waters (Del Castillo and others, 2000).

Aeolian deposition is an important source of nutrients to the West Florida Shelf. West Florida Shelf summer iron concentrations, for example, are controlled by not only local riverine inflows but also by windborne dust transported from Saharan Africa. This episodic dust supply can fuel significant diazotrophic (nitrogen-fixing) activity and, ultimately, red tides (Lenes and others, 2008).

The West Florida Shelf is a "leaky coastal margin" where submarine groundwater discharge (SGD) plays an important role. Many submarine springs occur along the West Florida Shelf, and SGD may be a significant source of nutrients, radionuclides, and other materials (Burnett and others, 1990). Groundwater inputs of nitrogen to the inner West Florida Shelf may at times exceed those from atmospheric and riverine sources and may have been largely responsible for the sustenance of an intense 2005 red tide (67,500 km^2) that could not have been supported by river runoff alone (Hu and others, 2006). Groundwater-related fluxes remain a significant unknown.

Phototrophic benthic microalgae are a potentially significant ecological constituent of the West Florida Shelf. Pelagic algal blooms of the West Florida Shelf can, upon decay and remineralization, contribute to the growth of these members of the shelf-sediment flora. The contribution of phototrophic benthic microalgae to continental shelf ecosystems and carbon cycling has only recently been appreciated (Darrow and others, 2003).

Northern Gulf of Mexico

The northern Gulf margin (figs. 1, 4) is a highly dynamic, river-dominated region strongly influenced by watershed dynamics, most notably via Mississippi River inflow. Sediments on this shelf are largely terrigenous (land derived), and the region bears the distinction of annually developing one of the world's most spectacular hypoxic zones ("the dead zone").

The Mississippi River is the world's second longest (6,700 km). Its basin, which covers 4,141 m of vertical relief, 6 degrees of latitude, and approximately 3.72 million km^2, is the world's second largest, draining nearly 14% of North America and more than 40% of the continental United States.

Mean precipitation is 94 cm/yr (Brown and others, 2005), ranging from 60 cm/yr in the northern grasslands to 160 cm/yr in the south (DeLong, 2005). Food and fiber crops (such as corn, soybeans, rice) dominate the southern vegetation. For the basin as a whole, land use is 57% agricultural, 28% forest/shrub, and 14% urban (Brown and others, 2005). The agricultural lands are generally highly engineered, characterized by pesticide and fertilizer application and physical modifications (for example, tilling) to facilitate the use of heavy machinery (Raymond and others, 2008). Population density in the upper basin is 54 individuals/km^2; in the lower basin, it is 10 individuals/km^2 (Brown and others, 2005; DeLong, 2005). Mean river discharge to the Gulf is 18,400 m^3/s, with runoff peaking in April (Brown and others, 2005). The Mississippi River is the major nutrient source to the Gulf, and its sediment discharge rate is among the world's top 10 (Pennock and others, 1999). The basin exports about 10 (±5) grams of carbon per square meter per year ($gCm^{-2} y^{-1}$) (80% in the form of dissolved inorganic carbon, DIC) to the Gulf, largely from cultivated land, where erosion is an order of magnitude greater than on forested land (Raymond and others, 2008).

Significant discharge from the Mississippi, in conjunction with the Atchafalaya River, is responsible for relatively high terrestrial inputs of organic carbon compared to other coastal margins of the United States (Hedges and Parker, 1976; Bianchi and others, 1997). Recent work has suggested that much of the terrestrially derived organic carbon delivered to the shelf is from C_3 and C_4 plants and materials from eroded soils in the northwestern grasslands of the Mississippi River drainage basin. These investigators also concluded that C_4 plant material [^{13}C-enriched values similar to marine organic carbon (MOC)] was transported greater distances offshore because of its characteristically smaller grain size (Goñi and others, 1997; Goñi and others, 1998; Onstad and others, 2000; Gordon and Goñi, 2003). On the basis of earlier work, Goñi and others (1997) concluded that the C_3 (^{13}C-depleted) terrestrial samples were being deposited on the shelf. However, recent analyses suggested that woody angiosperm material (C_4-depleted) preferentially settles within the lower Mississippi and in the proximal portion of the dispersal system on the shelf (Bianchi and others, 2002). More recently, it has been demonstrated that erosion of relict peats in transgressional facies of the lower Mississippi River can provide another source of "old" vascular plant detritus to the Louisiana coastal margin (Galler and others, 2003). Inputs of *Spartina* spp. (C_4 plants) from eroding marshes are also sources that contribute to the C_4 signal found in Louisiana shelf sediments.

The Mississippi River Delta is one of the most modified aquatic coastal ecosystems in the world and experiences as much as 80% of the wetland loss nationwide (peak rates of 60-90 km^2/y) (Gagliano and others, 1981; Turner and Rabalais, 1991). Overall, recent estimates indicate an annual flux of particulate organic carbon (POC) of 9.3 x 10^8 kilograms per year ($kg y^{-1}$) to the Gulf of Mexico (Bianchi and others, 2007). Total lignin fluxes, which were based on lignin content normalized to organic carbon values of POC, were estimated to be 1.2 x 10^5 $kg y^{-1}$. Louisiana shelf sediments have also been shown to effectively record the decrease in sediment and POC accumulation since about 1952, due to dam construction in the river (Allison and others, 2007). If the total DOC flux is included (3.1 x 10^9 $kg y^{-1}$) (Bianchi and others, 2004; Bianchi and others, 2007), this results in a total organic carbon flux of 4.0 x 10^9 $kg y^{-1}$. This represents 0.82% of the annual total organic carbon supplied to the oceans by rivers (4.9 x 10^{11} kg).

Other major rivers in the region include the Choctawhatchee, Escambia-Conecuh, Mobile, Pascagoula, and Pearl. Their drainage basins are characterized by a moderate climate and abundant rainfall, and their mainstem channels are often fragmented by damming and deepened by dredging. Several of the major rivers flow into moderate to large estuaries (Pennock and others, 1999).

The river-dominated estuaries that characterize the northern Gulf from the Florida panhandle to eastern Texas have short residence times, some as low as 2 days (Solis and Powell, 1999), and high displacement rates (Pennock and others, 1999). These high displacement rates indicate the potential for substantial discharge of materials to the Gulf and enhancement of shelf productivity (Solis and Powell, 1999). Gulf bays dominated by freshwater inflow (such as the Atchafalaya-Vermilion Bay) show little intra-annual variability in salinity, unlike most GMx estuaries (Solis and Powell, 1999). Among U.S. Gulf estuaries, salinity values tend to be lowest in the vicinity of the Mississippi River (Solis and Powell, 1999). Galveston Bay's Port of Houston is one of the world's busiest commercial ports. In 2006, it recorded more than 7,500 vessel calls (Port of Houston Authority, 2008).

Tides are dominantly diurnal on Alabama shores, strongly diurnal at the Mississippi River Delta, and mixed in Louisiana (Flick and others, 2003). Tidal range at Pensacola, FL, is 0.40 m; at Galveston, TX, it is 0.36 m (Stumpf and Haines, 1998).

The northern Gulf of Mexico acts as a "continental integrator." This region integrates a huge meridional range because of the size and location of its watershed. The Mississippi River drains more than 3 million km^2, approximately 40% of the land area of the continental United States, and supplies about 90% of the GMx freshwater inflow (Mitsch and others, 2001).

The northern Gulf margin is strongly influenced by watershed/river processes and land use in the continental United States. Efforts to reduce the development of hypoxia in the northern Gulf, for example, focus in large part on changing agricultural practices in the Mississippi River basin (Mitsch and others, 2001).

Because conditions in the northern Gulf are determined in large part by river processes, river management represents an important nexus where some control over fluxes can be exerted. Policy and management decisions can impact water quality on surprisingly short time scales.

River plume processes profoundly influence carbon fluxes and cycling in the northern Gulf. The Mississippi River supplies the shelf not only with freshwater but also with large amounts of dissolved and suspended particulate materials. Primary production rates in the Mississippi River plume are among the highest measured in large-river estuaries and plumes (Cai, 2003), and plume waters are distinct from those of the Gulf at large in terms of air-sea gas exchange. Offshore transport of plume sediments to canyons is important in GMx carbon transport.

The northern Gulf in the region of the Mississippi River plume may be an important CO_2 sink. Studies suggest that biological productivity fueled by nutrient input can lead to seawater in this region becoming a strong local CO_2 sink during the summer growing season (Chavez and others, 2007).

The northern continental shelf has the largest zone of oxygen-depleted shelf waters ("the dead zone") in the western Atlantic Ocean. Its extent on the sea bottom (1996-2006 average) is twice the total surface area of the Chesapeake Bay (Turner and others, 2007). Hypoxia is one symptom of eutrophication—an increase in carbon production and accumulation rates—and improved carbon-flux monitoring is a primary recommendation of the U.S. Environmental Protection Agency's Scientific Advisory Board (U.S. EPA, 2007). The annual formation of this northern GMx low-oxygen water mass (Rabalais and others, 2002) profoundly affects not only local biotic assemblages but also sediment structure and all chemical constituents and biogeochemical cycling in the area.

This province provides a good opportunity to study cross-shelf sediment/carbon transport, including the roles of benthic and canyon-related processes. The northern Gulf experiences massive sediment input, and its submarine canyons are relatively accessible. Sediment remobilization is an important process in this area.

The northern Gulf supports major recreational and commercial fisheries. The Mississippi River region supports one of the United States' most productive fisheries (Pennock and others, 1999), with fisheries in the northern Gulf generating $2.8 billion per year (NOAA, 2007). With estuarine-dependent species accounting for more than 95% of the commercial GMx fish harvest, area wetlands (more than half the U.S. total) (U.S. EPA, 1999) constitute a significant commercial asset.

This region is the site of much of the Gulf's hydrocarbon production. The outer continental shelf of the Gulf of Mexico, with its nearly 40,000 wells, is said to be the world's most extensively developed and mature offshore petroleum province (Kaiser and Pulsipher, 2007).

Western Gulf of Mexico

The northwestern Gulf (figs. 1, 4) is fed by 11 major rivers with generally narrow southeast-trending catchments (the Sabine, Neches, Trinity, San Jacinto, Brazos, Colorado, Lavaca, Guadalupe/San Antonio, Nueces, and Rio Grande). The lower reaches of these rivers are generally channelized for irrigation and navigation. From east to west, the climate is increasingly arid, ranging from humid continental in eastern Texas to desert in western Texas. The western rivers contribute relatively little discharge to the Gulf (Dahm and others, 2005). Laguna Madre, one of the world's few hypersaline estuaries, is in this area (Solis and Powell, 1999).

The major river system of the western Gulf (figs. 1, 4) is the Rio Pánuco, which drains 98,200 km², mostly from the mountains of east-central Mexico (basin relief is 3,800 m), and discharges at the port city of Tampico. Mean air temperature is 20 °C, and mean precipitation is 96 cm/yr. Population density in the basin is low, and land use is dominated by traditional slash-and-burn and other agriculture in the uplands and sugar-cane and citrus farming and cattle ranching in the lowlands. Petroleum extraction also occurs in the lower basin. Water quality is poor in many places. Mean discharge to the Gulf is 540 m³/s (Hudson and others, 2005). The microtidal Estuario Pánuco is, most of the time, a highly stratified salt-wedge estuary (Arcos-Espinosa and others, 2008).

Much of the land/sea boundary in this region is defined by extensive sandy barrier beaches. The narrow shelf is characterized by anticyclonic ring interactions, convective mixing, and river runoff and fronts (Escobar-Briones and Soto, 1997). Tides are dominantly diurnal (Flick and others, 2003).

Coastal land use and land cover in this region are rapidly changing. For the six Mexican states bordering the southern and western Gulf, more than 80% of their economic activities—primarily oil and gas production and petrochemical industries, fisheries, marine transportation, agriculture, cattle ranching, and tourism—are located in or are associated with the coastal zone (Sánchez-Gil and others, 2004). Growing commercial and recreational activities on the Gulf's western coast are contributing to growing pollution problems (Siemens and others, 2006), with the Rio Pánuco being acutely compromised by water quality degradation (Hudson and others, 2005). Mexico's principal Gulf port is located at Veracruz (Siemens and others, 2006).

Episodic rivers with high sediment loads flow into this Gulf region. The major river system, the Rio Pánuco-Tamesi, arises in the arid altiplano, descends through dry mountains and moist forests, and enters the Gulf near Tampico. Discharge is low from December through May and often peaks in September, following regional patterns of precipitation, which are determined in part by tropical cyclones (Hudson and others, 2005).

The western Gulf is characterized by strong eddy/ shelf interactions. Loop Current warm core rings have been observed colliding with the western shelf (Oey and others, 2005). Shelf properties and benthic communities in the area are strongly influenced by these ring interactions (Escobar-Briones and Soto, 1997).

Summer coastal upwelling occurs in this region. Upwelling-favorable winds occur from April to August, peaking in July. As a result, cold waters occur on the shelf in the summer, with maximum sea surface temperatures occurring in September (Zavala-Hidalgo and others, 2006).

Longshore and cross-shelf transport are both important on this narrow shelf. At Veracruz, the shelf is only about 30 km wide (Zavala-Hidalgo and others, 2006).

The northwestern Gulf of Mexico is characterized by vast rafts of free-floating vegetation. Satellite ocean color studies (2002-2007) indicate that *Sargassum*—a protected essential fish habitat and a huge carbon pool—accumulates in the Gulf early in the year, with concentrations peaking May-June. The floating brown algae is then advected into the Atlantic, occurring off Cape Hatteras in the summer and eventually northeast of the Bahamas by the following February (Gower and others, 2006; Gower and King, 2008). Sea surface accumulations of *Trichodesmium* are also prominent in the northwestern Gulf.

Southern Gulf of Mexico

The major river system of the southern Gulf (figs. 1, 4) is the Usumacinta-Grijalva, which drains a 112,600 km^2 region characterized by tropical rain forest. Basin relief is 3,800 m. Mean air temperature is 23 °C, and mean precipitation is 199 cm/yr (Hudson and others, 2005). The low-lying Tabasco Plain is one of the regions of highest Gulf coast rainfall (Solis and Powell, 1999). Population density is approximately 28 individuals/km^2. Dominant land cover is forest (59%) and cropland (31%). Mean discharge to the Gulf is 2,678 m^3/s, with runoff peaking in October (Usumacinta only) (Hudson and others, 2005). Tides in this region are dominantly diurnal (Flick and others, 2003).

The watershed data for the southern Gulf of Mexico represent a significant knowledge gap. In general, fewer data are available for Mexican watersheds, rivers, and marine areas than for regions in the United States. Water quality information for the Usumacinta-Grijalva River system, for example, is not available (Hudson and others, 2005). The Campeche Bay/ Bank area, a broad tropical carbonate platform that hosts some of the Gulf's healthiest coral reefs, has long been recognized as a strategic location for a global-observing network time-series station (IOC, 1997).

The Usamacinta-Grijalva River system, which drains lush tropical rain forest, provides the second highest fresh-water discharge to the Gulf, second only to the Mississippi (Yáñez-Arancibia and Day, 2006). All of the drainage basin receives ample rainfall. Discharge into the Gulf is poorly quantified (Hudson and others, 2005).

One major uncertainty in the region is associated with groundwater fluxes. Submarine groundwater discharge into the Yucatan coastal zone is significant (Álvarez-Góngora and Herrera-Silveira, 2006) but poorly quantified. The semiarid lagoons of the karstic northern peninsula receive very little surface inflow but significant groundwater discharge from submarine springs. This groundwater tends to be character-ized by low suspended sediment, low dissolved oxygen, low ammonium and phosphate, and high nitrate concentrations (Pennock and others, 1999). In the state of Quintana Roo on the Yucatan Peninsula, groundwater pollution is a major concern (Yáñez-Arancibia and Day, 2006).

The southern coastal region is experiencing rapid population growth. The state of Quintana Roo, for example, has experienced exponential population growth over the last quarter-century, driven largely by tourism (Yáñez-Arancibia and Day, 2006).

With this rapid population growth come rapid changes in land cover, land use, and the delivery of continental materials to the Gulf. In Quintana Roo, for instance, an explo-sion of tourism has brought cruise ships and extensive coastal development. The result has been widespread inland deforesta-tion, groundwater pollution, coastal habitat destruction, and unsustainable fisheries (Yáñez-Arancibia and Day, 2006). Biomass burning is also significant in the region. For the six Mexican states bordering the southern and western Gulf, more than 80% of their economic activities—primarily oil and gas production and petrochemical industries, fisheries, marine transportation, agriculture, cattle ranching, and tourism—are located in or are associated with the coastal zone (Sánchez-Gil and others, 2004).

Cross-shelf exchange is important in Campeche Bay. The southern shelf, with the exception of the huge Campeche Bank, is generally narrow.

The Yucatan is one of the most important upwelling regions on a western oceanic margin (Merino, 1997). One upwelling area has been observed north of Cabo Catoche (IOC, 1997), a site of high new carbon production and chlo-rophyll stocks. A second upwelling area has been observed as a band of cool coastal water along the northern Yucatan coastline (IOC, 1997).

The Campeche area experiences nearly year-round phytoplankton blooms and may export red tide "seed" material to other areas of the Gulf. On the Bank of Campeche, diatom blooms occur in the winter and spring, followed by toxic dinoflagellate blooms during summer and fall. Bloom material is often entrained into the Loop Current, which carries it north and east into the Gulf of Mexico (IOC, 1997).

The southern Gulf is the site of significant hydro-carbon production. The Bay of Campeche is responsible for more than three-quarters of Mexican oil and gas production (Schifter and others, 2005).

Gulf-Wide Features

Some important processes and research opportunities are common to all five Gulf provinces.

Sea-Level Rise. The entire Gulf of Mexico is subject to global sea-level fluctuations. Additionally, local geomorphology and processes that contribute to high rates of relative sea-level rise (SLR) make some margin areas especially vulnerable. During the past century, mean sea level has risen consistently in the Gulf of Mexico (Stumpf and Haines, 1998). For the U.S. Gulf Coast, lowest rates of SLR (0 to 3 mm/yr) are found along the Florida coast, and highest rates (upwards of 9 mm/yr) are found in eastern Louisiana (NOAA, 2008). The microtidal range of the entire Gulf Coast enhances vulnerability to the effects of rising sea level (Thieler and Hammar-Klose, 2000).

Most of the eastern Gulf is at moderate risk in terms of vulnerability to sea-level rise. The greatest risk factors in this region are its geomorphology (largely high-risk barrier island complexes, marshes, lagoons, and deltas), low tidal range and, in some areas, high erosion rates (Thieler and Hammar-Klose, 2000).

In the northern Gulf, relative (local) sea level is rising in some areas at rates of up to 10 mm/yr. Coastal erosion and wetlands loss along the northern Gulf are occurring at dramatic rates. In the Mississippi Delta, annual wetlands loss may be as high 65 km^2 (Douglas, 2005).

In some areas of the southern Gulf (Campeche), the sea is advancing inland at about 3 m/yr (IOC, 1997). Campeche coastal areas are characterized by extensive seagrass meadows, mangrove forests, tidal wetlands, and a broad deltaic environment (Yáñez-Arancibia and others, 1999)—low-lying or shallow environments susceptible to drowning or inundation by rising seas.

Extreme Events. The region is subject to extreme natural events. The warm waters of the Caribbean and Gulf provide abundant energy to fuel intense tropical storms (Maloney and Hartmann, 2000), and the entire Gulf region is subject to hurricanes and the accompanying extreme precipitation and devastating storm surge and high winds. High precipitation associated with cold fronts constitutes an additional hazard in some areas.

The northern Gulf region provides a good opportunity to study the effects of extreme events on a river-dominated ocean margin. This region is subject to a variety of short-term, intense environmental disruptions, such as hurricanes and river floods. The northern continental slope experiences turbidity currents and debris flows. The distribution of existing research facilities along the northern Gulf makes a regionally coordinated research response to extreme events feasible (Bortone, 2006).

The western Gulf margin and its watersheds are subject to droughts and floods. Some of the flood risk is associated with tropical cyclones. In August 2007, Hurricane Dean made landfall (its second) just north of Veracruz as a Category 2 storm (Avila, 2008). River flow in the region tends to be flashy, following local precipitation (Hudson and others, 2005).

Along the southern margin, one of the most devastating recent events was associated with the passage of a cold front. In late October 2007, high precipitation and Grijalva River overflow inundated the Tabasco lowlands, generating extensive infrastructure and property damage and impacting more than 1 million victims (López-Méndez and others, 2008).

Ocean Acidification. Since 1980, approximately one-third of the excess CO_2 released by anthropogenic activities has been taken up by the oceans. This uptake, which tends to drive seawater to lower pH and lower carbonate-mineral saturation states, is expected to increase carbonate dissolution rates, decrease biotic and abiotic calcification, and perhaps shift the average composition of modern carbonate sediments (Kleypas and others, 2006; Morse and others, 2006). Corals are expected to become increasingly rare in response to the double blow of a warming climate and ocean acidification (Hoegh-Guldberg and others, 2007).

The "carbonate factory" of the broad West Florida Shelf in the eastern Gulf represents significant buffering capacity and provides a natural subtropical laboratory for studying ocean acidification. Situated in the subtropical transition zone between photozoan-reef communities (coral reefs characterized by photosynthesis-dependent aragonitic corals and calcareous algae) and heterozoan-ramp carbonate communities (carbonate ramps characterized by foraminifers and coralline algae), this shelf offers a good opportunity to study changes in aragonite saturation state and carbonate-producing biota (Hallock, 2005). Such studies are needed to understand and predict the responses of shallow-water carbonate communities to conditions of rising atmospheric CO_2.

The southern region's carbonate-producing communities provide another natural laboratory—this one more tropical in nature. Campeche Bank, like the West Florida Shelf, is a sedimentary carbonate environment but is more tropical in nature. Coral reefs, almost a third of the Gulf's named reefs, occur on this broad bank. Largely removed from human and continental influence by their distance offshore, these reefs are among the healthiest in the area (Tunnell, 2007). Whitings also occur in

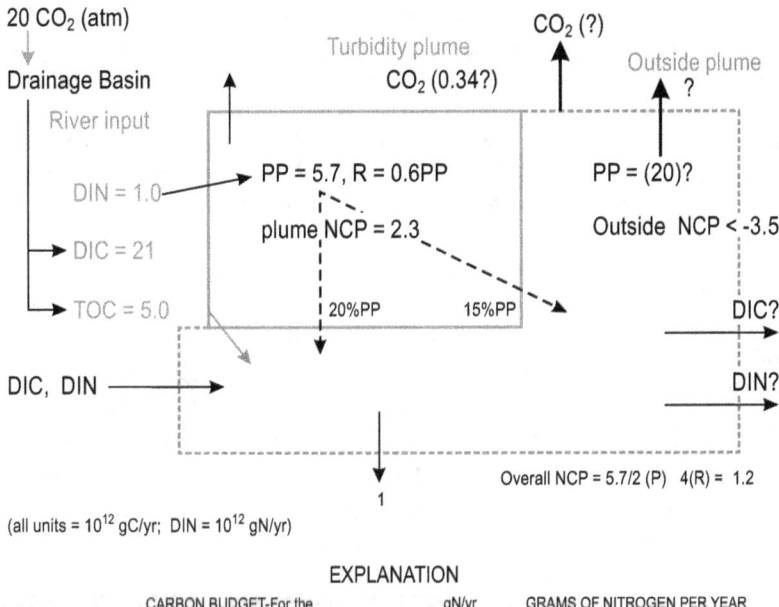

(all units = 10^{12} gC/yr; DIN = 10^{12} gN/yr)

EXPLANATION

	CARBON BUDGET-For the	gN/yr	GRAMS OF NITROGEN PER YEAR
―――――	Mississippi River plume	NCP	NET COMMUNITY PRODUCTION
---------	northern Gulf of Mexico	P	PHOTOSYNTHESIS
DIC	DISSOLVED INORGANIC CARBON	PP	PRIMARY PRODUCTIVITY
DIN	DISSOLVED INORGANIC NITROGEN	R	RESPIRATION
gC/yr	GRAMS OF CARBON PER YEAR	TOC	TOTAL ORGANIC CARBON

Figure 5. Carbon budget for the Mississippi River plume (green box) and northern Gulf of Mexico. Courtesy of Wei-Jun Cai.

the region. The socioeconomic impact of declining fisheries habitat including coral reefs (Orr and others, 2005; Fabry and others, 2008) may be especially severe in this region.

International Collaboration. Research in the Gulf of Mexico provides an ideal opportunity for international collaboration. Three countries have watersheds bordering the Gulf of Mexico—the United States, Mexico, and Cuba. Activities in any one of these countries' watersheds can potentially affect the industries—such as fisheries, oil, and tourism—and welfare of the others.

Carbon Budgets and Fluxes

Achieving closure of macroscopic carbon budgets in continental margin settings is generally difficult (Hales and others, 2008), and the Gulf of Mexico is no exception. The key unresolved questions regarding carbon cycling along North American margins (Hales and others, 2008) apply to the Gulf as well: Is the coastal ocean a net source or sink for atmospheric CO_2? What are the net sources and forms of carbon and nutrients delivered from rivers through estuaries to the ocean? What is the net processing of terrestrial and marine carbon within the coastal ocean, and what are the resulting net transfers of carbon between the coastal oceans and adjacent areas (for example, coastal seafloor, open ocean)? In other words, the fluxes of total carbon across key interfaces are poorly constrained, and the net diagenesis of total carbon in the coastal ocean is poorly understood.

At present, no carbon budget is available for the Gulf of Mexico as a whole or for most GMx subregions. Preliminary budgets for the northern Gulf shelf, site of the Gulf's dominant river system, have been recently formulated, still with large uncertainties (fig. 5; Lohrenz, 2008; Lohrenz and Cai, 2008; Cai, unpub. data, 2008). This exercise, useful for identifying not only major flux terms but also major data gaps, should be undertaken for the Gulf early in a GMx carbon research program, along with direct measurements of fluxes across key interfaces.

The major GMx carbon pathways are terrestrial inputs; vertical flux, sinking, and burial; shelf-ocean exchange; and air-sea flux. Significant carbon-transformation processes in the Gulf include primary production, remineralization and biogeochemical cycling, and photodegradation/photoremineralization (Lohrenz, 2008). Major uncertainties in GMx carbon budgets include the rates of organic carbon degradation in the water column and surface sediments and the rates of shelf-ocean carbon exchange (Lohrenz and Cai, 2008; Lohrenz, 2008).

Terrestrial inputs of inorganic and organic carbon to the Gulf of Mexico arrive primarily via rivers on the northern and southern GMx shelves. Estimated terrestrial input to the northern Gulf from the Mississippi-Atchafalaya River system is approximately 26.0 teragrams of carbon per year (TgC/yr) (fig. 5). Roughly 80% arrives in the form of inorganic carbon, almost all dissolved, and 20% arrives as organic carbon (8% dissolved plus 12% particulate). For comparison, total riverine carbon input to the global ocean is approximately 50% dissolved inorganic carbon and 50% organic carbon (28% dissolved plus 22% particulate; McKee, 2003; Lohrenz, 2008).

Mississippi River organic carbon export (5.0 TgC/yr) represents more than 10% of the total POC+DOC export for North America (as estimated by Seitzinger and others, 2005). Even in areas where the delivery of organic carbon is not particularly large (such as the West Florida Shelf), its implications for ecosystem structure and carbon cycling can be significant (Walsh and others, 2003).

Several lines of evidence indicate significant recent changes in terrestrial inputs to Gulf waters. The riverine supply of inorganic carbon, for example, has increased over recent decades in the northern Gulf (Raymond and Cole, 2003). During the past half-century, the export of carbonate alkalinity ($HCO_3^- + CO_3^{2-}$) from terrestrial soils to the Gulf via the Mississippi River has increased dramatically, due in part to increased river flow (resulting from higher rainfall in the river basin) and in part to changes in land cover. Alkalinity export per unit area tends to be high in areas of cropland cover.

Groundwater represents another route for terrestrial inputs and can be significant, especially along the eastern (Corbett and others, 2000; Hu and others, 2006) and southern shelves. Even in areas without conspicuous springs, groundwater inflow via seepage can be important (for example, northern and northeastern Gulf; Cable and others, 1996; Krest and others, 1999; Rutkowski and others, 1999). Submarine groundwater discharge into Gulf coastal regions has not, however, been extensively studied (Zektser and others, 2007). The role of coastal wetlands as suppliers of organic carbon ("outwelling") is also emerging as an important GMx research issue (Lohrenz, 2008).

GMx vertical carbon flux, sinking, and burial are highly variable in space and time, and large uncertainties are associated with their estimates. Rivers deliver large amounts of particulate and dissolved organic carbon to GMx estuaries and shelves, but the fractions recycled in the water column, recycled in surface sediments, exported to the open ocean, and buried in sediments are not well known (Lohrenz and Cai, 2008). In situ marine production is also an important source term.

In general, water-column degradation of POC in shallow, river-dominated areas is relatively small compared to that occurring in the open ocean (with its long settling times), but in some shelf areas adjacent to the Mississippi River, pre- and post-depositional decay can be equally significant (Chen and others, 2001; McKee and others, 2004). Sinking of particulates (Trefry and others, 1994), flocculation and aggradation (Dagg and others, 1996), and zooplankton-mediated vertical transfer (Wysocki and others, 2006) are important and have been best studied in the northern Gulf. Vertical flux rates of organic material may also be enhanced by lithogenic particles that act as ballast materials (Trefry and others, 1994). High sedimentation rates encourage longer-term organic carbon burial and preservation (McKee and others, 2004; Lohrenz, 2008; Lohrenz and

Cai, 2008). Organic carbon burial on the northern Gulf shelf is estimated to be approximately 0.5 to 1.0 Tg/yr (approximately 10-20% of the terrestrial delivery; Lohrenz, 2008).

Shelf-ocean exchange is perhaps the most poorly constrained flux term for the Gulf. Important GMx shelf-exchange processes include eddy-topography interactions (Sutyrin and others, 2003), buoyancy-driven circulation, wind-driven canyon flow (Yuan, 2002), river-plume displace-ment, and circulation and upwelling. Upwelling patterns in the Gulf are influenced by not only winds but also bottom bathymetry (see Weisberg and others, 2000). Wind forcing also exerts a strong influence on the position of the Mississippi River plume and the transport of suspended sediments (Walker and others, 2005). In areas of high deposition, sediment mass movement (for example, slumps and slides in the vicinity of the Mississippi; McKee and others, 2004) is significant.

Limited observations, comparisons with similar systems, and preliminary calculations indicate that, on an annual basis, the Gulf is likely a source of CO_2 to the atmosphere (fig. 3) (Chavez and others, 2007; Lohrenz and Cai, 2008). Local exceptions have been observed on the eastern and northern shelves in association with high biological produc-tivity, which can produce significant CO_2 drawdown (see Lohrenz and Cai, 2006). On the eastern shelf, nearshore sampling indicates that surface waters are a CO_2 source, but it is not known whether these sites are representative of the broader shelf. The state of the northern, western, and southern shelves is not known. In the area of the Mississippi River plume, surface partial pressure of carbon dioxide (pCO_2) is highly variable (Chavez and others, 2007; Lohrenz, 2008; Lohrenz and Cai, 2008), with reduced pCO_2 consistently observed in late spring and early summer (Lohrenz and Cai, 2006; Lohrenz, 2008). Resolving the magnitude of the Gulf of Mexico CO_2 source (or sink) is a critical need (Chavez and others, 2007; Lohrenz and Cai, 2008).

Developing general expectations or predictions regarding CO_2 fluxes in the Gulf is difficult, as key forcings in the region can drive surface pCO_2 toward either super- or under-saturation (Lohrenz and Cai, 2008). Rivers, for example, deliver significant organic matter to the Gulf—the respiration of which tends to elevate pCO_2. At the same time, rivers also deliver freshwater (buoyancy) and nutrients, which encourage water column stratification and fuel photosynthetic CO_2 uptake—thus lowering surface pCO_2. Storms can similarly create conditions that support both CO_2 release to the atmo-sphere and CO_2 uptake. For example, storms may destratify the water column and bring high-pCO_2 waters to the sea surface, where they can outgas to the atmosphere. But storms may also, through more than one pathway, deliver nutrients that support post-storm blooms and CO_2 uptake.

Additional GMx observations are needed to improve estimates of CO_2 air-sea exchange and other carbon-related fluxes for North American coastal oceans and the continental atmosphere. No large-scale systematic effort to measure air-sea CO_2 fluxes has been undertaken in the Gulf (Lohrenz and Cai, 2008), and maps of coastal surface water pCO_2 measurements show few in the region (fig. 2). Limited data are available for the relatively well-studied eastern and northern shelf areas, with additional data collected recently on the 2007 NACP Gulf of Mexico and East Coast Carbon Cruise (GOMECC) (Peng and Langdon, 2007). For the western and southern shelves, no measurements of CO_2 distributions or fluxes were unearthed during recent data compilations (Chavez and others, 2007; Lohrenz and Cai, 2008). A full complement of seasonal pCO_2 measurements is also lacking (Chavez and others, 2007). For the entire Gulf, not a single $1° \times 1°$ pixel has CO_2 measurements for more than two calendar months (see fig. 1.4 in Hales and others, 2008).

Gulf CO_2 fluxes are important in the modulation and estimation of continental (atmospheric) CO_2 concentrations, especially for the U.S. mainland north of the Gulf of Mexico. Large fluctuations in air-sea CO_2 fluxes—not uncommon in the coastal ocean—can influence CO_2 concentrations over adjacent continents. This effect is especially important where the mean airflow is onshore, as is typical of the summertime northern GMx coast. In addition, poorly characterized air-sea CO_2 fluxes and variability can introduce significant errors into continental CO_2 fluxes calculated by atmospheric inversion methods, especially at regional scales (Chavez and others, 2007; Hales and others, 2008; Lohrenz and Cai, 2008).

Estimating and explaining GMx carbon fluxes and budgets requires consideration of not only carbon but also carbon-relevant elements and compounds (such as nutrients) and ecosystem structure. In the Mississippi plume, for example, river-supplied nutrients support high levels of biological production, which in turn strongly influence particle export fluxes and air-sea CO_2 exchange (Lohrenz and Cai, 2008). Integrated primary production (Lohrenz and others, 1997; Cai and Lohrenz, in press) and satellite-derived chlorophyll measurements (Lohrenz and Cai, 2006) are directly proportional to terrestrial nitrogen fluxes. Sustained high nutrient loading from the Mississippi River also drives sustained high sedimentary oxygen demand (Turner and others, 2008), which profoundly influences the cycling of carbon and many other elements on the northern shelf. The Mississippi River not only dominates the terrestrial input of nitrogen and phosphorus to the Gulf (Turner and Rabalais, 2004)—it is also unique among the world's major rivers, having the highest ratio of dissolved inorganic nitrogen (DIN) flux to discharge (Dagg and others, 2004).

In northern Gulf plume and marine food webs, the largest fluxes of carbon are through the phytoplankton and bacterioplankton. The major fate of phytoplankton is microzoo-plankton-dominated grazing (Lohrenz, 2008), but grazing and "packaging" by larger zooplankton (for example, copepods) may have a greater impact on vertical carbon fluxes (Dagg and others, 2007).

Gulf of Mexico carbon modeling studies, an important tool in budget formulations, are in an early stage of development. Ocean circulation models have been developed for the Gulf, with a particular focus on the challenge of reproducing Loop Current behavior, and ecosystem models have been developed for the study of specific regions and ecological components (for example, red tides on the West Florida Shelf; Walsh and others, 2003). However, carbon cycling in the Gulf of Mexico has never been modeled (Hales and others, 2008). Early experimental efforts are now underway (He, 2008), coupling ecosystem models (see Denman and Peña, 1999; Fennel and others, 2006; Kishi and others, 2007) with a U.S. East Coast and GMx circulation model.

From Drainage Basin to Ocean Basin: Research Gaps, Linkages, and Opportunities

The Gulf of Mexico is uniquely well suited for the study of land/ocean coupling as it influences carbon fluxes and biogeochemical cycling. The landward boundaries of the Gulf are best defined not by its tidal shores but by the upslope and recharge boundaries of its watersheds and aquifers (fig. 1). Many rivers, submerged springs and seeps, and atmospheric exchange processes link the Gulf to the lands and people of the North American continent. Freshwater, sediments, nutrients, and carbon—inorganic and organic, particulate and dissolved, labile and refractory—are supplied in great quantity to the semi-enclosed basin, and the Gulf's warm waters in turn supply moisture and sustenance to the midcontinental United States and other Gulf regions.

Critical data/research gaps

- Long-term monitoring data
- Direct observations of total carbon and related fluxes across key ocean interfaces
- Community ocean circulation model

Rigorously defined high-quality physical and biogeochemical measurements will be required to constrain estimates of carbon inputs, transport, transformation, and fate in the streams, rivers, estuaries, and open basin of the Gulf of Mexico. The various forms of carbon, nitrogen, and phosphorus need to be better understood and more skillfully measured. Methods development and investment in new technologies will be key elements of a successful GMx program. Particulate organic carbon measurements, for example, need to be improved (compelling evidence of measurement shortcomings is presented in the fact that some databases report more dissolved than total organic carbon), and spectral information about dissolved components would be helpful. The capabilities of isotope and optical measurements (such as fluorescence) have yet to be fully exploited.

Key observations regarding GMx carbon sources, transport, and sinks include characterizations of seasonal carbon storage in river channels, suspended minerals and organics in watersheds and coastal environments, river nutrient inputs, groundwater-ocean interface fluxes, cross-shelf and canyon sediment transport, and storm and frontal-event impacts (for example, flushing of coastal systems and resuspension of sediments).

The major sources of terrestrial carbon to the estuaries, shelves, and central basin of the Gulf of Mexico are not well characterized. Both riverine and nonriverine sources supply significant carbon, but the relative contributions of the various sources are not well known, nor are the relative proportions of various carbon forms or the effects of tides, seasonality, and coastal management. Nonriverine sources include aeolian deposits as well as runoff (including stormwater runoff) and seepage from wetlands, coastal lagoons, marshes, beaches, and groundwater. In the Gulf basin, contributions from natural hydrocarbon seeps and oil platforms are also of interest.

Long-term precipitation and river discharge monitoring are critically needed, and recent cutbacks in these programs are a concern. Precipitation, along with land use/land cover, is a key determinant of carbon fluxes from the landscape into streams and estuaries and ultimately the Gulf. Data on area-specific precipitation are needed, as are better constraints on likely precipitation-pattern changes associated with large-scale climate change. Understanding fluxes through river-mouth and estuarine zones is a key need, for which the coverage of stream gage monitoring stations will need to be expanded downstream into the zone of tidal influence (into the salt wedge).

Comparative studies of the contrasting river-estuarine systems of the Gulf of Mexico are encouraged. For example, Mexican GMx watersheds and rivers have generally fewer dams and greater rainfall than U.S. watersheds, and that contrast presents an opportunity to study the effects of a range of landscape processes. To help characterize fluvial contributions to the Gulf, determination of the carbon loading of a variety of GMx rivers over time would be helpful. Much of the research to date has focused on the northern Gulf because of the magnitude of the signal there and the relevance of carbon loading to the problem of hypoxia (see Turner and others, 2007). Riverine carbon storage and downstream transport in general are not well understood, nor are connections to higher trophic levels. Improved definition of the stream-flow network is required, and accumulation terms need to be defined, along with in-stream residence times and downstream changes in nutrient reactivity. In river-dominated areas, a better under-

standing of the importance of in-river autochthonous production below the confluence relative to upstream watershed and tributary inputs is needed. Quantification of the effects of dams and land use changes on riverine carbon transport and sequestration around the Gulf is essential.

Recommendations

- Reinstate key monitoring stations and programs and support their long-term maintenance
- Quantify fluxes of carbon and carbon-relevant materials across key interfaces via direct measurement with accompanying process studies
- Identify the major sources of terrestrial carbon to the Gulf

Groundwater inputs, which are poorly characterized but substantial in at least the eastern and southern regions, cannot be ignored. In some areas, groundwater flow dominates the freshwater inflow (Pennock and others, 1999). This inflow—the significance of which is coming to be appreciated by not only scientists but also coastal managers—can be an important source of freshwater, carbon, nutrients, pesticides, industrial wastes, sewage, and pathogens (SCOR and LOICZ, 2004).

The role of GMx wetlands needs to be better constrained. Preliminary results from one case study in northern Gulf salt marshes, for example, indicate that outwelling and ground-water inputs of DOM likely exceed riverine inputs in the area (Dittmar, 2007). Inferences from studies of the microbial food web may also indicate a role for wetlands-derived DOM in encouraging the development of hypoxia (Dagg and others, 2008). A major data gap is the lack of a nationally consistent wetlands database (Boyer, 2008); wetlands characterizations are inconsistent in their approach and need to be standardized. Remote sensing can likely contribute to this endeavor.

The nature of the carbon discharged to the Gulf, refractory versus labile, needs to be better characterized, as do the effects of changing proportions as the carbon is processed in estuaries and on the shelf. In the northern Gulf, the relative proportions of labile and refractory carbon have tremendous societal relevance, as different assumptions or conclusions regarding the lability of terrestrial carbon leads to starkly different conclusions regarding the cause of inner-shelf hypoxia—and therefore strikingly different mitigation recommendations (Boesch, 1999, 2003). Fluorescence measurements suggest that Mississippi River DOC is more labile than the DOC of Florida rivers, yet this difference and its implications have yet to be fully explored.

The fate of carbon once it enters the coastal ocean is not well understood. Lateral and vertical carbon fluxes need to be quantified, but the dominant modes and effects of carbon transformation and transport are not well characterized. It is not known, for example, how much terrigenous organic carbon is remineralized in the water column, how much is remineralized in the sediments, or how much is buried and preserved in estuarine, shelf, slope, and basin environments (Lohrenz and Cai, 2008). The fate of carbon discharged to the Gulf depends in large part on the type of margin to which the materials are delivered (for example, shallow, shelf-dominated versus deeper, slope-dominated). Variations in river flow, biological production, remineralization, photochemistry, hydrological sorting (winnowing), and diagenesis must all be considered (Gardner and others, 1994; Waterson and Canuel, 2008). Carbon-relevant species—their fluxes and biogeochemical cycling—must be considered as well. Nitrogen cycling in general (including N supply and N_2 fixation) is a critical topic (Lohrenz, 2008).

Recommendations

- Support community development and adoption of a mature GMx ocean circulation model
- Support continuous, well–calibrated satellite ocean color measurements; support algorithm development for sea-surface temperature, sea-surface salinity, chlorophyll concentration, phytoplankton standing stock, and colored dissolved organic material

---

Sediments are very important in Gulf estuaries yet also represent a major unknown in terms of their dynamics and biogeochemical roles (for example, in modulating biological productivity or delivering pollutants). Approximately 90% of the sediment discharged by rivers of the conterminous United States enters Gulf estuarine environments (McKee and Baskaran, 1999).

The role of inorganic (mineral) ballast on carbon transport in the Gulf is likely significant but is not well characterized. The association of nearly neutrally buoyant organic particles with dense, fast-sinking mineral particles allows the organic matter to sink at an accelerated rate. This association may also help preserve the organic matter from degradation (Armstrong and others, 2001; Lee and others, 2004). Candidate mineral ballast particles in the Gulf include fine terrigenous river-borne sediments, aeolian dust particles, siliceous diatom tests, and the calcium carbonate tests of foraminifera.

Determination of transport parameters for dissolved species presents a particular challenge, and the quantity of terrigenous carbon transported offshore as dissolved organic carbon remains unknown. Research in the northern Gulf indicates that autochthonous production, bacterial utilization, and photo-oxidation could all be important in regulating and removing DOC. Further study of these processes is recommended (Wang and others, 2004).

The role of microbial organisms and food-web processes represents a major knowledge gap. Recent work in the northern Gulf, for example, indicates that the microbial food web may make an unexpectedly significant contribution to the summertime development of inner-shelf hypoxia when pelagic appendicularians are abundant in coastal waters, especially during times of low river flow and in regions remote from the Mississippi-Atchafalaya River plumes (Dagg and others, 2008).

The effects of episodic events, including their timing and frequency, warrant further investigation. These effects are sometimes dramatic and sometimes subtle. In the disappearing salt marshes of the undeveloped northern Gulf, for example, spectacular hurricanes are the dominant supplier of inorganic sediment, with the net long-term effect being greatest when several strong hurricanes occur within a few years (Turner and others, 2007). On the Campeche shelf of the southern Gulf, quiet changes in the local macrofauna of carbonate sediments accompany winter storms coming from the northerly direction, as evidenced by increases in opportunistic polychaete taxa several months after storm passage (Hernández-Arana and others, 2003).

Another important issue is the transport and fate of river-, wetland-, and plume-derived material across the shelf to canyons. In the river-dominated northern Gulf, the slope and canyons may be important sinks for terrigenous carbon (Waterson and Canuel, 2008). Ultimate GMx carbon sinks (such as burial, export) and controls on burial rates are in general poorly quantified.

Other significant unknowns include the role of photochemistry, effects of hypoxia on carbon burial, effects of salt wedge adsorption/desorption processes, and the role of events beyond GMx boundaries (that is, south of Yucatan). The land-sea exchange of living resources (for example, the cycling of shrimp, fish) is an open question to which fisheries data might be applied.

Gulf of Mexico air-sea gas fluxes are of intense interest, but observations are sparse. The Gulf remains largely unsampled and poorly characterized in terms of air-sea gas exchange (figs. 2, 3). Extrapolation from limited CO_2 data collected primarily on the northern and eastern shelves suggests that Gulf and Caribbean waters are, on an annual basis, a CO_2 source (Chavez and others, 2007). Extrapolation from other limited data—those collected in the southern Gulf and Caribbean Sea—suggest the opposite: that the region is a

CO_2 sink (Wanninkhof, 2008). To better characterize regional CO_2 fluxes, a network of surface water pCO_2 observing systems (ships and moorings) is recommended.

Recommendations

- Establish surface water pCO_2 observing systems (ships and moorings)
- Establish a robust air sampling program
- Perform a process study for direct measurement of CO_2 fluxes (as an example, a yearlong platform study)
- Develop robust CO_2-relevant remote sensing algorithms applicable to regions affected by riverine input

---

A more extensive CO_2 dataset is needed to characterize not only GMx air-sea fluxes but also regional land-atmosphere fluxes. Atmospheric inversion approaches to estimating net regional land-atmosphere exchanges rely in part on carbon dioxide measurements in surface seawater. At present, open ocean values are used because coastal ocean data are generally not available. This compromised approach may result in the misattribution of some regional fluxes, especially in zones with large area-specific air-sea CO_2 fluxes and mean cross-shore air flow, such as the summertime northern Gulf (Hales and others, 2008). Preliminary analyses (Wanninkhof, 2008) indicate that air CO_2 values used in inversion models may be lower (by about 2 parts per million) than actual Gulf values. High-quality air measurements are needed in coastal (land and sea) areas.

The Gulf is potentially important in the exchange of not only carbon dioxide but also other climatically active gases. The open ocean, estuaries, and coastal seas can be important sources of such gases [Upstill-Goddard, 2006; for example, carbon monoxide (CO) and methane (CH_4)], but exchange rates are not well quantified in the Gulf of Mexico or other coastal waters.

Estimation of air-sea gas fluxes presents a particular challenge in coastal waters (Upstill-Goddard, 2006). Gas exchange processes are complex, and spatial and temporal gradients in coastal areas are strong. Seawater pCO_2 and gas exchange are influenced by ocean circulation, primary production, mineralization, and a host of other atmosphere and ocean processes and properties, some of which may be specific to the coastal ocean—that is, strong salinity and alkalinity gradients, terrigenous carbon supply, high turbidity, eutrophication, benthic processes, suboxic respiration, and pollutants (Liu and others, 2000).

In the open ocean, calculations of air-sea gas exchange are often based on measurements of wind speed (from which gas-transfer velocities are derived) and observed differences in air and surface-water pCO_2 values. However, the 1996 Florida Shelf Lagrangian Experiment (FSLE) (Wanninkhof and others, 1997) and other studies have shown that this approach can yield inaccurate results in coastal regions (see Zappa and others, 2003; Baschek and others, 2006; Tokoro and others, 2007). Therefore, direct eddy covariance air-sea flux measurements (McGillis and others, 2001a) or indirect measurements using tracers (Wanninkhof and others, 1997) or the gradient flux method (McGillis and others, 2001b) would be a useful part of any Gulf of Mexico carbon study. A process study for direct measurement of CO_2 fluxes (for example, a yearlong platform study) is recommended.

Potentially important factors in the Gulf of Mexico include the effects of chemical enhancement, biofilms, surface ocean density fronts, and wave fetch. Carbon dioxide is not an inert gas, and its air-sea exchange rates may be enhanced by its chemical reactions in seawater under conditions of low turbulence and high pH (Morel and Hering, 1993; Wanninkhof and Knox, 1996). In equatorial areas, with low winds and high temperatures, chemical enhancement has been calculated to account for 4-8% of the total CO_2 exchange (Wanninkhof and Knox, 1996). The subtropical Gulf of Mexico is also characterized by low winds and relatively high temperatures.

Biofilms may also be important in the Gulf, tending to suppress gas exchange. These organic materials may act as surfactants and can substantially reduce rates of gas transfer across the air-sea interface (Azetsu-Scott and Passow, 2004). Laboratory studies of oxygen evasion rates under turbulent conditions have documented rate reductions of 5-50% in the presence of phytoplankton exudates (Frew and others, 1990).

Fronts, which are common in the Gulf of Mexico, may be sites of enhanced air-water gas transfer. Strong turbulence and bubble entrainment typically occur in conjunction with frontal downwelling (Marmorino and Trump, 1996), enhancing gas transfer in ways not captured by wind-based parameterizations (Baschek and others, 2006). In the northern Gulf, fronts are common due to strong buoyancy input from the Mississippi River.

Wind fetch can also be important in influencing GMx sea state and therefore gas exchange. Gas transfer velocities increase with greater fetch (Zhao and others, 2003) and greater whitecap coverage (Monahan and Spillane, 1984; Wanninkhof and others, 1995).

Strong spatial and temporal variability, typical of coastal waters, further complicate experimental design and data interpolation and extrapolation. River plumes, for example, though relatively limited in areal extent, may exert strong local effects on air-sea gas exchange. In the vicinity of the Mississippi River plume, spatial CO_2 gradients and air-sea differences can be quite large (Cai and others, 2008).

Priority research questions related to Gulf CO$_2$ exchange cover a great range of temporal and spatial scales and range in scope from basic characterizations of seawater chemical distributions to studies of potentially far-reaching GMx influences on continental airmass chemistry. Air sampling programs and surface observations of seawater pCO$_2$ are a high priority. The vertical distribution of CO$_2$-system species in Gulf waters is also largely unknown and should be included in sampling programs. Determination of air-sea CO$_2$ fluxes in the coastal seas of the conterminous United States is a component of the North Atlantic Carbon Program.

The effects of eddy variability and other physical processes (such as upwelling and downwelling) on CO$_2$ source/ sink behavior in the Gulf merit additional study. Seasonal and episodic events (examples include hurricanes and diatom blooms) may induce rapid system changes from source to sink or vice versa, and the effects need to be better understood. Episodic wind events, for example, can produce coastal upwelling that drives rapid air-sea gas exchange (see Lueker and others, 2003). Coastal upwelling is known to contribute to the Gulf's highly variable CO$_2$ levels and correspondingly variable CO$_2$ fluxes (Wanninkhof and others, 2007).

Many pressing questions about Gulf carbon dioxide fluxes relate to biologically mediated processes. For example, what is the role of GMx primary production as a sink for atmospheric CO$_2$? High nutrient input, as seen in the Mississippi River delta region, contributes to pCO$_2$ drawdown (Wanninkhof, 2008). What other elemental cycles are important in controlling CO$_2$ fluxes? The effects of nitrogen fixation, denitrification, and calcification by marine organisms need to be better characterized. Recently, anammox reactions have been found to represent a surprisingly significant pathway for the loss of fixed nitrogen in low-oxygen natural waters. The role of this process in the anoxic zone of the northern Gulf is a tantalizing unknown (Arrigo, 2005).

Meteorological processes play an important role in moving atmospheric constituents between continental and marine areas (Parrish and others, 1992), and GMx ocean-continent fluxes through the atmosphere are an important research topic. The Mississippi River plume, due to its large area and strong air-sea gradients, may influence ocean-continent atmospheric fluxes. In the Gulf, the transport of volatile organic compounds (VOCs) and the effects of atmospheric pollution plumes are of particular interest.

The implications of human practices (such as land use and river flood control) for Gulf of Mexico carbon fluxes cannot be ignored. Large-scale societal changes in Mexico and the United States have profoundly affected Gulf conditions, and such changes can be expected to continue and in some cases accelerate. During the 1900s, for example, changing agricultural practices in the Mississippi River basin (such as tile drainage, fertilizer use, irrigation, tillage practices, and changes in crop type) led to increases in river discharge. In conjunction with increased precipitation and agricultural lime applications, the net result has been a large increase in alkalinity flux, which in turn has implications for many other element and biogeochemical cycles (Raymond and others, 2008). Mississippi River Delta sediments also record depositional changes during that time consistent with documented historical changes in upriver land use (such as deforestation), damming, and channelization (Santschi and others, 2007). Restoration plans like those proposed for the Florida Everglades are also likely to produce major changes in carbon and nutrient fluxes to the Gulf (NRC, 2002).

With more land within Gulf watersheds now going "under the plow," land use changes will have a profound influence on future Gulf conditions. In the United States, Conservation Reserve Program (CRP) enrollments are declining, as land is being converted from conservation to agricultural uses, largely in response to shrinking global food surpluses and anticipated increases in biofuel demand. Large-scale, rapid landscape changes can be expected, with the net effect being the conversion of terrestrial nitrogen to Gulf carbon. The effects of increasing biofuel production, in particular, may be profound. One GMx management goal is to reduce the application of nitrogen (as fertilizer) in upstream watersheds. However, cropland conversion from soy to corn production, as is being encouraged by anticipated ethanol demand, requires the application of additional nitrogen. The current expansion of corn-based ethanol production in the Midwest and the resulting increase in nitrogen export is expected to make nearly impossible the hoped-for reduction of the northern GMx hypoxic zone unless large shifts in food production and agricultural management are implemented (Donner and Kucharik, 2008).

Climate change introduces another major unknown for the Gulf of Mexico. There remains considerable uncertainty regarding likely future temperature and especially precipitation over GMx watersheds—climate conditions that will ultimately influence watershed carbon yields. One particular difficulty in predicting the terrestrial supply of carbon to Gulf coastal and ocean regions arises from the large uncertainties in climate-change predictions for the Mississippi River basin (Najjar, 2008). Large uncertainties are also associated with how climate change is likely to affect soil nutrient stores and weathering rates. The community acknowledges the importance of constraining precipitation predictions.

Summary: Common Themes and General Recommendations

An integrated, three-pronged approach to the study of Gulf of Mexico carbon fluxes is recommended, utilizing field observations, remote sensing, and coupled physical-biogeochemical modeling. Some of the most pressing questions regarding net fluxes of total carbon across key interfaces can be addressed directly through the development of a coastal ocean observing system. Such a system would include both direct CO_2-system measurements and supporting measurements (such as radioisotopes). Ocean buoys, flux towers, dedicated research cruises, and ships of opportunities are all important platforms for making CO_2 flux measurements at critical interfaces (air-sea, land-ocean, land-air). Paleo-oceanography and paleoclimatology provide an important complementary perspective.

Remote sensing, which has radically transformed our understanding of ocean processes in recent decades, will play an extremely important role in GMx carbon studies. The development and improvement of remote sensing algorithms for the characterization of sea surface temperature (SST), sea surface salinity (SSS), chlorophyll concentration, phytoplankton standing stock, colored dissolved organic material (CDOM), and dissolved organic carbon (DOC) would be especially useful. The possibility of a lapse in well-calibrated ocean color measurements is a grave concern.

Numerical models are an essential complement to observational programs and should be used to help design observation systems, plan effective field campaigns, and interpret results. A nested system of coupled physical-biogeochemical models with data assimilation capabilities should be implemented in conjunction with the field programs. Adoption of a community circulation model should be a core undertaking. Support for the development of complementary models (producing high-resolution salinity fields, for example) is encouraged.

Judicious integration of field observations, remote sensing, and numerical modeling provides a powerful and essential tool for data interpolation and extrapolation, integration, and interpretation. Another potential application is the use of remote sensing to generate synoptic CO_2 flux maps of larger areas than can be achieved by field sampling alone. A good example of an integrated interdisciplinary modeling, data assimilation, and analysis project is the U.S. Eastern Continental Shelf Carbon Budget (U.S. ECoS) program (Hofmann and Mannino, 2007). A similar program should be an integral part of a coordinated Gulf of Mexico carbon study. The Gulf of Mexico carbon project should strategically capitalize on existing data, infrastructure, and models.

Data Availability and Continuity

A formal data-mining effort should be initiated as soon as possible to compile existing datasets and identify critical data gaps. A Web-accessible forum should be provided to receive and distribute quality-controlled and quality-assured data. Funding for this substantial data compilation effort will be necessary in the initial stages of a Gulf of Mexico project.

Basic terrain data and long-term hydrological monitoring of U.S., Mexican, and Cuban GMx watersheds are critical to our understanding of biogeochemical cycles in the Gulf of Mexico. Initial data compilation and synthesis efforts should include the gathering of digital elevation models (DEMs) for Mexico and Cuba. The United States has uniquely robust continental-scale datasets (Sundquist, 2008), but a major data gap is the lack of a nationally consistent wetlands database (Boyer, 2008). National digital inventories of forests, land use, and ecoregions have been published for Mexico, and a forest update is scheduled for 2009 (Muhlia Melo, 2008). Gulf watershed information about not only land use but also land characteristics (such as soil mineral content) will be required. High-spatial-resolution data for continental carbon inventories (for example, biomass and soil carbon) are available.

Some long-term time-series datasets (as examples, flow regimes, historical land use, nutrient loadings) collected by academic, federal, state, and local agencies in Gulf regions need to be collated and intercalibrated. Standardization of units of measure and correction for methodological differences will be required.

Ongoing programs and data collection initiatives that will contribute significantly to GMx observational efforts are U.S. Department of Agriculture (USDA) land use data, National Aeronautics and Space Administration (NASA) satellite observations, National Oceanic and Atmospheric Administration (NOAA) ocean observing systems, and EPA and USGS water-quality data. Minerals Management Service (MMS) has an ongoing research program focused on the Gulf of Mexico (see *http://www.gomr.mms.gov/homepg/regulate/ environ/ studiesprogram.html*), as well as an online Report Archive (see *http://www.gomr.mms.gov/ homepg/regulate/environ/techsumm/ rec_pubs.html*). The U.S. Long-Term Ecological Research (LTER) network offers an additional source of valuable data.

These varied background data are needed to assess such things as the likely flux-related impacts of changes in land use and land cover, the stability of erosion control measures, and the extent and effects of sustainable land use practices. Integration of these historical and new datasets will contribute greatly to the ability to model and predict key carbon fluxes in river-estuary systems, including air-sea CO_2 flux, lateral exports to the shelf, and carbon sequestration in sediments.

Continuity of data collection, in terms of both frequency and duration, is a critical element of a successful Gulf of Mexico research program. Long-term historical datasets are necessary for model implementation, validation, and calibration, and the procurement of adequate funding for this core element is essential.

Of particular concern regarding continuity of data:

☐ USGS stream-gaging station data: Fewer rivers and streams are monitored today than in 2000 (U.S. EPA, 2007).

☐ Satellite ocean color data: The potential for a lapse in well-calibrated ocean color measurements is a particular concern.

☐ Remote sensing algorithm development: Field observations required to support the development of remote-sensing algorithms must be adequately supported.

Recent declines in stream-gaging and water-quality monitoring programs will hamper efforts to monitor, model, and predict likely impacts of many terrestrial and aquatic processes related to GMx carbon fluxes. During the 1990s, the number of U.S. river gages dropped by about 6%; between 1971 and 1999, gages on small, free-flowing rivers dropped 22% (Stokstad, 1999). Declines since then have continued (U.S. EPA, 2007). It is imperative that discontinued monitoring stations be re-established, that current stations be maintained, and that networks be expanded. These long-term data, along with new types of data, are required to validate the numerical models upon which scientific advances depend and upon which policy decisions will be based.

Gulf of Mexico studies would benefit greatly from a geostationary ocean color satellite, such as the proposed GEO-CAPE mission (NRC, 2007). This mission would provide data on aerosols, phytoplankton, organic matter, suspended sediments, and other constituents of ocean color at frequencies of several passes per day, thus permitting direct observation of dynamic, short-time-scale events and processes. In situ field observations and measurements are essential for the development of remote sensing algorithms, ocean color and otherwise.

The selection of GMx study sites should be chosen by using existing classification schemes and study sites—such as those of the international Land-Ocean Interactions in the Coastal Zone project (LOICZ) or the U.S. National Estuarine Research Reserve System (NERRS). In the United States, the National Ecological Observatory Network (NEON) (Keller and others, 2008) may be an especially good partner in this regard. The lack of study sites in aquatic systems in the North American Carbon Program (Ogle and Davis, 2006) must be redressed immediately.

Additional sampling opportunities (for example, ships of opportunity) should be explored as a means of expanding Gulf data coverage. Complementary platforms might include commercial shipping vessels, pleasure cruise ships, and hydrocarbon-extraction ships and platforms.

Meteorological and military towers represent one potential opportunity for building on existing infrastructure and encouraging coordinated cross-disciplinary research:

☐ U.S. Air Force towers - Roughly half a dozen of these unused military towers are located along the west Florida coast and could potentially be instrumented for GMx studies.

☐ Tall towers - Meteorological tall towers sample atmospheric parameters at heights of tens or hundreds of meters and give a "footprint" view on the scale of hundreds of kilometers. At present, only a few North American tall towers exist.

☐ Flux towers - Flux towers measure the exchanges of CO_2, water vapor, and energy between terrestrial ecosystems and the atmosphere, and their sites are well characterized in terms of vegetation, soil, hydrologic, and meteorological characteristics. The United States has active flux towers in Florida (Everglades and Gainesville) and Texas (San Marcos) and inactive towers in Florida and Mississippi. Mexico's one active flux tower is located in the mountains of La Paz (*http://public.ornl.gov/ameriflux/site-select.cfm*). Long-term continuity of funding for flux towers is not assured (Baldocchi, 2008).

Numerical Modeling

Numerical modeling will be an essential component of a GMx carbon program and should be used to help plan effective field campaigns and interpret results. Fiscal realities inevitably limit the scope of field programs; therefore, a nested system of coupled physical-biogeochemical models with data assimilation capabilities (for both field and remote sensing measurements) should be implemented prior to and in conjunction with the field program. Historical data from the initial data-mining effort can be used to constrain existing models, which can in turn be "sampled" to help determine optimal scales and locations for observations. New data will be supplied to the models as they come available. For some carbon-relevant questions, modeling of a particular environment may be appropriate (such as certain river/estuarine systems). For other questions, an exploration of couplings and feedbacks among the atmosphere, terrestrial watersheds, river systems, margins, open Gulf of Mexico, or adjacent basins may be required. Increases in Gulf sea surface temperature may, for example, result in higher atmospheric water vapor concentrations and concomitant increases in precipitation over land—which will in turn influence GMx conditions.

Socioeconomic and climate-change aspects that may need to be considered in Gulf models include:

- Changes in land and water management (agricultural practices, human population distributions, groundwater mining, etc.)

- Changes in sea level, sea-surface temperature, and ocean chemistry (for example, ocean acidification; Kleypas and others, 2006)

- Changes in coastal morphology (for example, through subsidence or coastal erosion)

Quantifying model uncertainty—and therefore the precision and accuracy of the underlying field data—should be a core element of field and modeling programs. Estimates of uncertainty can help qualify predictions and guide the prioritization of future research and data collection. Postponing the modeling effort until the program's end is to be avoided.

A forum devoted to collaborative assessment of existing data, model capabilities, and potential barriers to model-linking and -coupling is recommended. Forum participants should include modelers and observationalists drawn from a wide variety of complementary geographic and computational areas of expertise. Early model assessments must consider not only data availability and model capabilities but also software compatibility and "language barriers" (such as different state variables, different data formats). Many existing carbon models do not strictly trace carbon but are driven by pertinent constituents that influence carbon, such as nutrients. A core undertaking of this assessment effort should be the identification of candidate community ocean circulation models for the Gulf of Mexico. Circulation models constitute the "backbone" of spatially explicit biogeochemical ocean models, and GMx circulation modeling is a particular challenge.

Linked, nested models are recommended, and existing GMx models provide a good starting point. A general modeling strategy would be to nest and link existing models of various subsystems or components (for example, watershed yield, air-sea exchange, coastal shelf processing). Many major subsystems can be characterized adequately with existing models—for example:

- SPARROW - SPAtially Referenced Regressions on Watershed Attributes, for modeling surface-water quality (*http://water.usgs.gov/nawqa/sparrow/*)

- SWAT - Soil and Water Assessment Tool, a river-basin-scale model for quantifying the impact of land management practices in large, complex watersheds (*http://www.brc.tamus.edu/swat/*)

- Terrestrial CO_2

- VOC

- TEM - Terrestrial Ecosystem Model, a process-based ecosystem model that describes plant and soil (non-wetlands) carbon and nitrogen dynamics (*http://www.cgd.ucar.edu/vemap/abstracts/TEM.html*)

Model nesting is recommended to accommodate the great range of process scales encountered in Gulf regions. In dry, low-productivity terrestrial areas, for example, coarse spatial and temporal resolution may be adequate. In other areas, finer scale resolution will be required. A loose coupling (linking) of subsystem models is also recommended, in which the output from one subsystem model provides the input for another. For example, output from the SWAT and SPARROW models may provide some input required by coastal and oceanographic biogeochemical models. In some cases, tighter coupling may be required. For example, climate models need to be coupled to process-driven land models so that feedbacks can be identified and explored. As a general approach, models need to at least loosely couple carbon with other important constituents.

The development of complementary data assimilation models should be encouraged. Such models do not include carbon as a state variable but instead provide output fields needed by carbon researchers. One example is the U.S. Navy's experimental real-time Intra-Americas Sea Ocean Nowcast/Forecast system (IASNFS) (Ko and others, 2003), which could potentially supply high-resolution salinity fields for the calculation of CO_2 fluxes. Such models offer a powerful tool for regional data interpolation and extrapolation.

Issues of Scale

The determination of appropriate temporal and spatial scales for field observations and modeling efforts depends on the nature of the biggest unknowns in the constraint of Gulf of Mexico carbon fluxes. The overarching spatial scale can be conceptualized as a two-part system: the GMx marine basin, plus all North American watersheds that discharge into the Gulf (fig. 1). The relevant temporal scales require measurement frequencies ranging from hourly to seasonal, with durations ranging from one to several decades. A comprehensive GMx research program will require a blend of high-resolution (high frequency, short duration, small area) and low-resolution (low frequency, long duration, large area) measurements.

Critical scales need to be defined for a variety of carbon-relevant processes, parameters, and provinces. An important question is what kinds of carbon species need to be measured in different ecosystems and at what scales. Smaller scales need to be understood if we are to anticipate and predict changes occurring on larger scales. Longer temporal scales are required for more detailed system analyses. The relative contributions of steady-state conditions versus episodic events also need to be investigated.

In general, a minimum set of carbon fluxes for a particular region or spatial scale (for example, entire Gulf of Mexico) should be defined in terms of the carbon species or carbon-relevant parameters to be measured. Researchers can then identify where adequate assessments are available and where additional ones are required—that is, they can identify what kind of data to collect (at what scale, frequency, and duration) to answer specific questions.

A standard list of measurements should be formulated, related to the scales under consideration. For example, one goal might be to establish Mississippi River fluxes at heads of passes. There, "choke points" are small, and daily sampling is feasible. In the Mississippi River plume, however, long-term daily measurements are not feasible, except by remote sensing. Some processes can be sampled intensively, some not—and overlap of scales should be sought where possible. Point stations and moorings can provide high-frequency data, which must be combined with satellite data and shipboard measurements for spatial integration. Autonomous underwater vehicle (AUV) measurements of DIC-system parameters are also evolving and may soon offer another means of spatial integration.

Continental data synthesis inevitably presents scaling challenges. Variability is tied to the scale of the system, and there is a need to capture episodic events but also integrate them. Researchers will inevitably grapple with the question of, in collapsing temporal scales and integrating, what an appropriate scale of inference is. Analysis at continental scales must include watersheds and aquifers, which can be characterized, in part, in terms of land use (agricultural, forested). Measurement platforms include satellites and tall towers. The temporal scale for point measurements will be daily to annual, but maintenance of the instrumentation for these sorts of measurements is a challenge. For stream and river measurements, gages provide water fluxes (hourly) and often include less frequent (weekly) measurements of water quality. One important goal is the derivation of robust relations between water flux and carbon parameters. Water quality measurements are important and temporal coverage of events is desired, but sufficient data coverage does not currently exist.

The Gulf presents its own scaling challenges, and it must be kept in mind that the Gulf is characterized by continuums of properties and processes rather than hard physical boundaries. Once semi-distinct, process-defined provinces are defined and conceptual boundaries are established (fig. 4), it becomes necessary to measure fluxes across them, and this undertaking will be particularly difficult for the margin-basin boundary. In general, more intensive sampling (that is, smaller spatial and temporal scales of measurement) will be required in margin regions than in the central Gulf.

One goal for a GMx carbon program would be the formulation of a well-constrained carbon budget (inflows and outflows). Such a budget will not provide a detailed mechanistic understanding of carbon-relevant processes, but it will provide critical insights into the fate of land-derived carbon in the GMx system. As examples, the most important carbon fluxes and desired temporal and spatial measurement resolutions are provided here for two GMx provinces.

The **eastern Gulf shelf** (fig. 4) provides a good example of a margin region. Five important fluxes were identified by workshop participants:

- Air-sea CO_2 flux: the desired temporal resolution in this province would be hourly, with decadal duration. Temporal resolution may be better defined with a nested approach, starting with high frequency (hourly) measurements and decreasing the frequency when and where feasible.
- Land-sea carbon flux: this flux can be mediated by water flux via rivers or groundwater. Critical measurements include DIC, DOC, POC, PIC, and nutrients. Required temporal resolution is hourly, with decadal duration.
- Benthic-pelagic flux: again, pertinent parameters are DIC, DOC, POC, PIC, and nutrients. The desired temporal resolution is seasonal, with flexibility for event-based coverage. Temporal duration is decadal.
- Margin-to-basin flux: required parameters include DIC, DOC, POC, PIC, nutrients, and radium isotopes (for time scale definition). The desired temporal resolution is weekly, with decadal duration.
- Net primary productivity and respiration: the desired temporal resolution is monthly, with event-based coverage when possible. Duration is decadal.

Additional considerations include the role and definition of river plumes (with boundary definitions based on salinity or a combination of salinity and geography), fluxes outside the plume "box" and estuary-ocean exchange, fluxes from the water column to sediments and the potential for carbon burial, and shallow-to-deep water exchange (at the basin scale or smaller). Uncertainties about boundaries and the potential contributions of satellites should be explored as well.

For the **deep GMx basin** (fig. 4), measurements at the circulation "choke points"—the Yucatan and Florida Straits—will be important in quantifying carbon fluxes in and out of the basin. The Loop Current and eddies (large but transient—up to a year in duration) are the dominant physical features in the basin. Three major fluxes were considered to be most significant:

- Air-sea CO_2 fluxes for the entire Gulf of Mexico: air-sea carbon fluxes show significant interannual variability, so seasonal sampling is needed. Sampling duration should be decadal.
- Water mass flux through the Gulf of Mexico: measurement parameters associated with this flux are DOC, DIC, PIC, POC, pCO_2, and nutrients. Measurement frequency should be seasonal, with decadal duration.
- Primary production: estimations of primary production in surface waters of the deep basin can be derived from satellite observations of chlorophyll-*a* concentrations (that is, ocean color). The relevant temporal scales are weekly to annual, with decadal duration.

Infrastructure and Integration

Integration of the many individual research efforts in the Gulf of Mexico will require strategic investments in infrastructure and could lead to a significant increase in our understanding of the cycling of carbon and carbon-relevant materials through land, atmosphere, river, estuarine, and ocean reservoirs. Infrastructure is taken to mean common shared resources for use by the research community in terms of an integrated measurement program, a data management center, modeling efforts, and outreach activities. The following six efforts are recommended:

- □ An integrated network of carbon monitoring stations on land and ocean, building on existing infrastructure and augmenting these capabilities where needed

- □ A regular set of process cruises in the Gulf of Mexico

- □ The development of improved algorithms for interpretation of satellite remote sensing products

- □ A shared integrated modeling effort that is connected to the measurement efforts

- □ The establishment of a Gulf of Mexico data management center to provide a "one-stop" connection to all measurement, modeling, and remote sensing products

- □ A common communication effort that uses existing networks and outreach opportunities to involve stakeholders and decisionmakers in the research efforts

These six recommendations are further detailed below.

The community seeks to initiate a networked system of monitoring stations in terrestrial and aquatic environments in the GMx region, where a large-scale, integrated system can be leveraged against numerous smaller, dedicated systems that are already in place. A set of time series stations with carbon-relevant measurements is recommended. Many of these exist in some form already; others will need some modification or augmentation to meet the needs of the GMx-wide study. Specific examples include buoys, platforms, river gaging stations, and flux towers that are currently outfitted—or could be outfitted at minimal cost—with necessary instrumentation. For example, key physical parameters such as wind, salinity, and temperature are available from some existing platforms, such as those operated by the National Data Buoy Center (NDBC; *http://www.ndbc.noaa.gov/*) but will need to be augmented with in situ carbon sensors. In addition, networks such as the tall tower and aircraft sites operated by NOAA's Earth System Research Laboratory would need to be expanded for adequate spatial and temporal coverage of this region. Many universities and government agencies have assets along the Mississippi River and coastal sites along the Gulf that can provide access and staging areas for time-series sampling efforts. Gulf of Mexico ocean observing systems that are already in place can be utilized for leveraging and infrastructure support [see *http://www-ocean.tamu.edu/GCOOS/System/gom.htm* for information on Gulf of Mexico Coastal Ocean Observing System (GCOOS)]. Offshore drilling platforms provide an excellent opportunity for leveraging existing infrastructure for scientific use, but the science community needs to work closely to align science goals with industry needs to succeed with this dual use. For the capture of extreme events (hurricanes), a few critical sites need to be outfitted with rugged instrumentation designed to "weather the storm." Regular meetings of a Gulf of Mexico infrastructure working group and further discussion of existing measurement efforts, common data quality standards, and evolving technologies are needed to establish this network.

A set of routine coastal process studies measuring carbon system properties, hydrographic properties, and nutrients would greatly contribute to the goal of better understanding the transport and transformation of carbon-relevant species throughout the system. As in the case of networked monitoring stations, governmental agencies (federal, state, tribal, local), universities, and other organizations already have several projects underway that are collecting some of these vital measurements. This region is also host to numerous research laboratories that can provide facilities and logistical support for field measurements and laboratory experiments. Dedicating time and resources to establish continuity among these studies (including coordinating sampling efforts, intercalibrating data, and merging datasets) will advance the success of the proposed GMx field campaign. Through a regular set of process studies and time series measurements, researchers can begin compiling the data required for a more complete understanding of the transport, transformation, and fate of carbon and other climate-critical parameters in the Gulf of Mexico.

Remotely sensed measurements from aircraft and satellites are also required for synoptic coverage of Gulf processes. These products will be used to bridge the gaps where field data cannot be collected and will assist in developing sampling strategies. Emphasis on improved coastal zone sensors (such as complete CODAR coverage), coordinated airborne coverage (for example, LIDAR), and improved satellite remote sensing coverage (increased spatial and temporal resolution) and algorithms (especially for chlorophyll, CDOM, and salinity) is needed to guide process studies and drive models more accurately. This effort will require coordinated ground-truthing of the satellite measurements during time-series and process studies. Finally, higher-resolution remote sensing data (< 1 km resolution) are necessary for studying coastal processes such as outwelling, sediment transport, and wetland losses.

Fusion of all data products will require an extensive, integrated modeling effort. Validation of models would be conducted via hindcasting, with the purpose of ultimately generating forecasting models to provide predictive capabilities for management issues—in particular, land use effects on watersheds (both upstream and downstream). These models can in turn provide valuable information to guide sampling strategies and maximize data and information output. Numerical modeling, including data assimilation, will also be necessary in designing the observing network and scaling up the results of process studies. Modelers and modeling capabilities need to be considered and integrated during the planning stages of the time-series network and process studies to maximize the efficacy of the measurement efforts and ensure maximum impact of modeling products.

Implicit in a networking of stations and field studies is the recognition that different strategies will be needed for the unique reservoirs of interest. Each research community offers distinct strengths that may be applicable to other communities as well. An example is the detailed North American forest inventory of the USDA—translating that type of database to an aquatic environment for an equivalent coastal inventory would be very useful. Implementing new approaches in different regimes may offer a wealth of carbon-relevant information. Such cross-disciplinary, cross-environment approaches may also encourage the development of better sampling strategies in regard to extreme weather events, a problem that has challenged all field researchers and has compromised numerous datasets. Such an endeavor would give researchers an unprecedented opportunity to work collaboratively across disciplines and geographic realms to constrain climate-critical carbon measurements.

Skillful data management will be required to handle the numerous large datasets that would be generated by a large-scale GMx field campaign. To assure the provision of accessible, high-quality data to end users, a central data repository will be needed, as will adherence to universal formats and standardized collection protocols. Coordination will be necessary between Ocean Carbon and Biogeochemistry (OCB) and the North American Carbon Program (NACP) data management offices. The end result of this management effort needs to be data products that are easily accessible, user-friendly, and transportable to geographic information system (GIS) programs. The envisioned data management center would also bring together historical data to facilitate studies of past changes and the generation of longer time series. These efforts will allow for extensive data mining and maximal usage of existing data.

Research conducted in the GMx region falls under the recommendations of two nationally recognized carbon cycle research programs aimed at coordinating existing and new carbon cycle science research programs: the North American Carbon Program (NACP) and the Ocean Carbon and Climate Change Program (OCCC). The NACP and OCCC, which are supported by the U.S. Global Change Research Program Carbon Cycle Science Program and the U.S. Climate Change Science Program, address the global carbon cycle research theme in the *Strategic Plan for the U.S. Climate Change Science Program* (2003). Both programs have recognized the need for international collaboration in carbon cycle and climate research activities. A GMx research campaign would require such coordination with the Mexican governmental agencies and universities.

The success of this type of endeavor depends on the successful communication of results to the public. There is a need to educate the public at all levels in carbon cycle biogeochemistry and its social and economic implications. Web-based tools, graphic interfaces, and museum displays can all contribute to this goal.

Involving stakeholders and decisionmakers in the research program, from the planning stages to the end products, is critical in generating the sorts of interactions between scientists and their ultimate audiences that will result in maximizing the use of science in policy-making decisions. Interactive discussions of science strategies, measurement protocols, modeling products, and predictions need to be "two way," rather than simply flowing from the science community outward to the public. Feedback from the public can be gathered via high-tech interactive outlets (for example, Internet, YouTube, video games) and participation in existing large-scale networks such as the Centers for Ocean Science Education Excellence (COSEE) and the Global Learning and Observations to Benefit the Environment (GLOBE) projects.

International collaboration between the United States and Mexico will further broaden the impact of research efforts. A strategic plan for communication and outreach is necessary for maximizing the impact of this coordinated research.

In summary, determination of the magnitude and distribution of carbon sources and sinks requires quantification of the reservoirs of carbon and carbon-relevant parameters as well as the biological, chemical, and physical processes that influence their spatial and temporal variability. A comprehensive Gulf of Mexico research initiative will provide better constraints on carbon fluxes and concentrations in and across key interfaces such as watersheds, the Yucatan Strait, the shelf break, the sediment-water interface, and the atmosphere through in situ measurements, multidisciplinary process studies, and modeling. By coordinating time series measurements, process studies, data management, modeling, and outreach efforts, the Gulf of Mexico research community can make a great leap forward in its understanding of the carbon cycle in the Gulf and the relevance of these results to the global carbon cycle.

Workshop Agenda

Tuesday, May 6, 2008

7:30	Registration and Continental Breakfast at the USGS (Posters can be put up immediately)
8:30	Introduction, Welcome, and Logistics Welcome by USGS and USF College of Marine Science Comments by program managers: NSF, NOAA, NASA, USGS, MMS Goals of Meeting - **Paula Coble** and **Lisa Robbins**
9:30	Plenary Talks, Carbon Cycle Land-Ocean Coupling - Processes, Fluxes, and Fates Session Moderator: **Wei-Jun Cai**
9:30	**Eric Sundquist**, USGS, From Carbon Footprint to Carbon Pathway: Carbon-Cycle Science at Crossroads
10:10	Break
10:30	**Ken Davis**, Pennsylvania State University, Land-Atmosphere Dynamics and Measurement of CO_2
11:10	**Tom Bianchi**, Texas A&M University. Anthropogenic and Natural Effects on the Biogeochemistry of Organic Carbon Cycling in a River-Dominated Margin: The Mississippi River System
11:50	Questions for presenters
12:00	Lunch and posters
1:00	Moderator: **Ben de Jong**
1:00	**Steve Lohrenz**, Gulf of Mexico Carbon Cycling
1:40	**Rik Wanninkhof**, CO_2 Flux Dynamics over the Gulf of Mexico

2:20	**Dick Feely**, Pressing questions and research needs from morning session
	Open discussion:
	    (1) Most pressing questions or hypotheses
	    (2) General ideas on how to test them

3:00	Break

3:15	Breakout Session 1: Assessing the state of knowledge on carbon transport and flux in each of the three segments of the land-ocean system. What do we know? What are perceived data gaps? See actual breakout questions in Workshop folder.
	Breakout groups:
	    1. River/ Estuary Group - Meet in Normile Room
	        Co-Chairs: **John Paul** and **Miguel Goñi**
	        Reporter: **Regina Easley**
	    2. Terrestrial/ Watershed Group - Meet in Breakout Room 1
	        Co-Chairs: **Simone Alin** and **Charles Perry**
	        Reporter: **Lori Adornato**
	    3. Ocean/Terrestrial/Atmospheric Group - Meet in Breakout Room 2
	        Co-Chairs: **Liz Gordon** and **Carlos Del Castillo**
	        Reporter: **Laura Lorenzoni**

4:40	Report from Breakout 1 back to Normile Conference Room
6:30-10:00	Dinner reception and posters on StarLite Cruise: Loading at 6:30 p.m., leaving at 7:00 p.m. from USF docks; map will be provided. Cash bar. Bring sweater.

Wednesday, May 7, 2008

7:30 Continental Breakfast

8:30 Update: **Paula Coble** and **Lisa Robbins**, Normile Conference Room

8:45 Plenary Talks
Moderator: **Lisa Robbins**

8:45 **Peter Raymond**, Yale, Watershed Carbon Cycle and Export

9:15 **Hobie Perry**, USDA Forest Service, National Inventories of Terrestrial Ecosystem
Carbon Stocks, Documenting Impacts of Resource Management on Watershed Carbon Dynamics

9:45 **Ray Najjar**, Penn State, Eastern U.S. Continental Shelf Carbon Budget: Modeling, Data
Assimilation, and Analysis

10:15 Break
Moderator: **Paula Coble**

10:30 **Beth Boyer**, UC Berkeley, Modeling Watershed Nutrient Fluxes

11:00 **Mead Allison**, UT Austin, Modeling Sediment Transport and Deposition on GM. Shelf

11:30 **Ruoying He**, NCSU, Physical Oceanography and Circulation of the Gulf of Mexico

12:00 Lunch and posters

1:15 **Ben de Jong** and **Arturo Muhlia Melo**, Update on Mexican Carbon Programs and Projects

1:30 Breakout Session 2: Pulling together a design for a future research project, taking into account
the scales of variability, infrastructure required and modeling framework for integration across
the system. See actual questions in Workshop folder.

Breakout groups:

1. Modeling and Prediction Group - Meet in Normile Room
Co-Chairs: **Barnali Dixon** and **Chris Anderson**
Reporter: **David Butman**

2. Infrastructure Group - Meet in Breakout Room 1
Co-Chairs: **Kathy Tedesco** and **Bob Chen**
Reporter: **Robyn Conmy**

3. Scales Group - Meet in Breakout Room 2
Co-Chairs: **Ron Benner** and **Nazan Atilla**
Reporter: **David John**

4:00 Summary Report back from Breakout 2 to plenary

6:00 Dinner on your own

Thursday, May 8, 2008

7:30 Breakfast

8:30 **Wei-Jun Cai**, Summary of Breakouts 1 and 2 and Discussion of new directions

9:00 **Brent McKee** and **Miguel Goñi**

1. Discussion of priority environments to focus research

* Coastal environments around the Gulf, including Cuba, Straits of Florida, West Florida Shelf, north-east shelf, Mississippi/Atchafalaya River region, Louisiana/Texas shelf, East Mexico shelf, Bay of Campeche, Campeche Bank and the Yucatan channel. Which environments will be most influenced by climate change (CO_2 in systems)?
*Where is there synergy with past or planned research projects?

2. Implementation and proposal planning

12:00 Adjourn

1:00- 5:00 Report write-up session: including organizers, session chairs, reporters, and involved students

Participant List

Meeting Leaders:

Paula G. Coble
University of South Florida
140 7th Ave. South
St. Petersburg, FL 33701
Phone: 727-553-1631
E-mail: pcoble@marine.usf.edu

Lisa Robbins
U.S. Geological Survey
600 4th St. South
St. Petersburg, FL 33701
Phone: 727-803-8747 x3005
E-mail: lrobbins@usgs.gov

Lori R. Adornato
SRI International
140 7th Ave. South COT 100
St. Petersburg, FL 33701
Phone: 727-553-3502
Fax: 727-553-3529
E-mail: Lori.Adornato@sri.com

Simone R. Alin
NOAA Pacific Marine Environmental Laboratory
7600 Sand Point Way NE
Seattle, WA 98115
Phone: 206-526-6819
E-mail: simone.r.alin@noaa.gov

Mead Allison
University of Texas Institute for Geophysics
10100 Burnet Rd.
Bldg 196, R2200
Austin, TX 78758-4445
Phone: 512-471-8453
E-mail: mallison@mail.utexas.edu

Christopher J. Anderson
Auburn University
3301 Forestry and Wildlife Building
Auburn, AL 36849
Phone: 334-844-1033
E-mail: andercj@auburn.edu

Nazan Atilla
University of Wisconsin-Madison
Dept. Atmospheric and Oceanographic Sciences-Center for Climate Research
1225 West Dayton St.
Madison, WI 53706
Phone: 608-890-0472
E-mail: atilla@wisc.edu

Phil Bass
EPA Gulf of Mexico Program
Bldg. 1100, Rm 232
Stennis Space Center, MS 39529-6000
Phone: 228-688-2356
Fax: 228-688-2709
E-mail: bass.phil@epa.gov

James E. Bauer
VIMS, College of William & Mary
P.O. Box 1346
Gloucester Point, VA 23062
Phone: 804-684-7136
E-mail: bauer@vims.edu

Ronald Benner
University of South Carolina
Dept. of Biological Sciences
Columbia, SC 29208
Phone: 803-777-9561
E-mail: benner@biol.sc.edu

Heather Benway
OCB Project Office
Dept. of Marine Chemistry and Geochemistry
Woods Hole Oceanographic Institution
MS 43
Woods Hole, MA 02543
Phone: 508-289-2838
Fax: 508-457-2161
E-mail: hbenway@whoi.edu

Thomas S. Bianchi
Texas A&M University
Dept. of Oceanography, 3146 TAMU
College Station, TX 77843-3146
Phone: 979-845-5137
Fax: 979-845-6331
E-mail: tbianchi@tamu.edu

Paula Bontempi
NASA Headquarters
Mail Suite 3B74
300 E St. S.W.
Washington, DC 20546
Phone: 202-358-1508
E-mail: paula.s.bontempi@nasa.gov

Elizabeth W. Boyer
School of Forest Resources and Penn State Institutes of Energy and the Environment
304 Forest Resources Building
Pennsylvania State University
University Park, PA 16802
Phone: 814-865-8830
E-mail: ewb100@psu.edu

Jay A. Brandes
Skidaway Institute of Oceanography
10 Ocean Science Circle
Savannah, GA 31411
Phone: 912-598-2361
Fax: 912-598-2310
E-mail: jay.brandes@skio.usg.edu

David E. Butman
Yale University
210 Prospect Street
New Haven, CT 06511
Phone: 203-577-9911
E-mail: david.butman@yale.edu

Robert H. Byrne
University of South Florida
College of Marine Science
140 Seventh Ave. South
St. Petersburg, FL 33701
Phone: 727-553-1508
Fax: 727-553-1189
E-mail: byrne@marine.usf.edu

Wei-Jun Cai
University of Georgia
Department of Marine Sciences
Athens, GA 30602
Phone: 706-769-1466
E-mail: wcai@uga.edu

Robert F. Chen
University of Massachusetts Boston
Environmental, Earth and Ocean Sciences
100 Morrissey Boulevard
Boston, MA 02186
Phone: 617-287-7491
E-mail: bob.chen@umb.edu

Robyn N. Conmy
University of South Florida
140 7th Ave. South
St. Petersburg, FL 33701
Phone: 727-692-5333
Fax: 727-553-1189
E-mail: rconmy@marine.usf.edu

William T. Cooper
Florida State University
Department of Chemistry & Biochemistry
Tallahassee, FL 32306-4390
Phone: 850-644-6875
Fax: 850-644-8281
E-mail: cooper@chem.fsu.edu

Reide Corbett
East Carolina University
Department of Geological Sciences
Graham Bldg.
Greenville, NC 27858
Phone: 252-328-1367
E-mail: corbettd@ecu.edu

Kenneth J. Davis
Penn State University
512 Walker Building
Department of Meteorology
University Park, PA 16802
Phone: 814-863-8601
E-mail: kjd10@psu.edu

Mike D. DeGrandpre
University of Montana
Department of Chemistry
Missoula, MT 59812
Phone: 406-243-4118
E-mail: michael.degrandpre@umontana.edu

Bernardus H.J. de Jong
El Colegio de la Frontera Sur
Carra Reforma KM 15.5
Ra Guineo 2da Sección
C.P. 86280
Villahermosa, Tabasco, Mexico 86280
Phone: +52-993-3136111
Fax: +52-993-3136110 ext. 3001
E-mail: bjong@ecosur.mx

Carlos E. Del Castillo
The Johns Hopkins University
Applied Physics Laboratory
11100 Johns Hopkins Rd.
Laurel, MD 20723
Phone: 240-228-8457
E-mail: carlos.del.castillo@jhuapl.edu

Barnali Dixon
University of South Florida
140 7th Ave. South
St. Petersburg, FL 34236
Phone: 727-873-4025
E-mail: bdixon@stpt.usf.edu

Kellie Dixon
Mote Marine Laboratory
1600 Ken Thompson Parkway
Sarasota, FL 34210
Phone: 941-388-4441
E-mail: lkdixon@mote.org

William Drennan
University of Miami, RSMAS
4600 Rickenbacker Causeway
Miami, FL 33149
Phone: 305-421-4798
E-mail: wdrennan@rsmas.miami.edu

Eurico J. D'Sa
Louisiana State University
Coastal Studies Institute
Dept. of Oceanography and Coastal Sciences
Baton Rouge, LA 70803
Phone: 225-578-0212
E-mail: ejdsa@lsu.edu

Regina A. Easley
University of South Florida
College of Marine Science
140 7th Ave. South
St. Petersburg, FL 33701
Phone: 727-278-1470
E-mail: reasley@marine.usf.edu

Richard A. Feely
PMEL/NOAA
7600 Sand Point Way N.E.
Seattle, WA 98115
Phone: 206-526-6214
E-mail: Richard.A.Feely@noaa.gov

Sonia C. Gallegos
Naval Research Laboratory
Ocean Sciences - Code 7333
Building 1009 A
Stennis Space Center, MS 39529
Phone: 228-688-4867
Fax: 228-688-4149
E-mail: gallegos@nrlssc.navy.mil

Wilford D. Gardner
Texas A&M University
3146 TAMU
Department of Oceanography
College Station, TX 77845-3146
Phone: 979-845-3928
Fax: 979-845-6331
E-mail: wgardner@ocean.tamu.edu

Miguel A. Goñi
Oregon State University
College of Oceanic and Atmospheric Sciences
104 Ocean Admin. Bldg.
Corvallis, OR 97331
Phone: 541-737-0578
E-mail: mgoni@coas.oregonstate.edu

Elizabeth S. Gordon
Fitchburg State College
160 Pearl Street
Fitchburg, MA 01420
Phone: 978-665-3083
E-mail: egordon3@fsc.edu

Peter Griffith
NASA GSFC / SSAI Code 614.4
Greenbelt, MD 20771
Phone: 301-614-6610
E-mail: peter.c.griffith@nasa.gov

Burke Hales
Oregon State University
104 Ocean Admin. Bldg.
Corvallis, OR 97331
Phone: 541-737-8121
E-mail: bhales@coas.oregonstate.edu

Emily R. Hall
Mote Marine Laboratory
1600 Ken Thompson Parkway
Sarasota, FL 34236
Phone: 941-388-4441 x327
E-mail: emily8@mote.org

Dennis A. Hansell
University of Miami
4600 Rickenbacker Causeway
RSMAS/MAC
Miami, FL 33149
Phone: 305-421-4078
E-mail: dhansell@rsmas.miami.edu

Ruoying He
North Carolina State University
2800 Faucette Drive
Raleigh, NC 27695
Phone: 919-513-0249
E-mail: rhe@ncsu.edu

Iuri Herzfeld
University of Hawaii
1000 Pope Road
Honolulu, HI 96822
Phone: 727-692-1473
E-mail: herzfeld@soest.hawaii.edu

Gary L. Hitchcock
University of Miami/MBF
4600 Rickenbacker Causeway
Miami, FL 33149
Phone: 305-421-4926
Fax: 305-421-4600
E-mail: g.hitchcock@miami.edu

David T. Ho
Lamont-Doherty Earth Observatory
61 Route 9W
Palisades, NY 10964
Phone: 845-365-8706
E-mail: david@ldeo.columbia.edu

Charles W. Holmes
U.S. Geological Survey
9103 64th Ave. East
Bradenton, FL 34202
Phone: 941-753-0050
E-mail: cholmes@usgs.gov

Markus Huettel
Florida State University
117 N Woodward Ave.
Tallahassee, FL 32306-4320
Phone: 850-645-1394
Fax: 850-644-2581
E-mail: mhuettel@ocean.fsu.edu

David E. John
University of South Florida
140 7th Ave. South
St. Petersburg, FL 33701
Phone: 727-553-1647
E-mail: djohn@marine.usf.edu

Paul O. Knorr
U.S. Geological Survey
600 4th St. South
St. Petersburg, FL 33701
Phone: 727-803-8747
Fax: 727-803-2032
E-mail: pknorr@usgs.gov

Charles W. Kovach
Florida Department of Environmental Protection
13051 North Telecom Parkway
Temple Terrace, FL 33637-0926
Phone: 813-632-7600 x329
Fax: 813-632-7663
E-mail: charles.kovach@dep.state.fl.us

Mingliang Liu
Auburn University
3301 Forestry and Wildlife Sciences Building
Auburn University
Auburn, AL 36830
Phone: 334-844-8061
E-mail: liuming@auburn.edu

Sherwood Liu
College of Marine Science
University of South Florida
140 7th Ave. South
St. Petersburg, FL 33701
Phone: 727-553-3922
E-mail: liu@marine.usf.edu

Steven E. Lohrenz
The University of Southern Mississippi
1020 Balch Blvd.
Stennis Space Center, MS 39529
Phone: 228-688-3177
E-mail: Steven.Lohrenz@usm.edu

Laura Lorenzoni
University of South Florida
140 7th Ave. South, KRC 3117
St. Petersburg, FL 33701
Phone: 727-553-3987
Fax: 727-553-1103
E-mail: laural@marine.usf.edu

Alexis Lugo-Fernandez
MMS-Gulf of Mexico
OCS Physical Sciences Unit (MS 5433)
1201 Elmwood Park Blvd.
New Orleans, LA 70123-2394
Phone: 504-736-2593
E-mail: alexis.lugo.fernandez@mms.gov

Lawrence M. Mayer
University of Maine
Darling Marine Center
193 Clarks Cove Rd.
Walpole, ME 04573
Phone: 207-563-3146
E-mail: LMayer@maine.edu

Brent A. McKee
University of North Carolina - Chapel Hill
UNC Department of Marine Sciences
449 Chapman Hall; Campus Box 3300
Chapel Hill, NC 27599-3300
Phone: 919-843-3604
E-mail: bmckee@unc.edu

Ralph N. Mead
University of North Carolina - Wilmington
Department of Chemistry and Biochemistry
601 South College Road
Wilmington, NC 28403
Phone: 910-962-2447
E-mail: meadr@uncw.edu

Richard Miller
East Carolina University
Department of Geological Sciences
101 Graham
Greenville, NC 27858
Phone: 985-285-6708
E-mail: richard.miller@alumni.duke.edu

Dong-Ha Min
The University of Texas at Austin
Marine Science Institute
750 Channel View Dr.
Port Aransas, TX 78373
Phone: 361-749-6743
E-mail: dongha@mail.utexas.edu

Siddhartha Mitra
East Carolina University
Department of Geological Sciences
101 Graham
Greenville, NC 27858
Phone: 252-328-6611
E-mail: mitras@ecu.edu

Willard S. Moore
University of South Carolina
701 Sumter St.
Department of Geological Sciences
Columbia, SC 29208
Phone: 803-777-2262
Fax: 803-777-6610
E-mail: moore@geol.sc.edu

Arturo F. Muhlia
CIBNOR, S.C.
Mar Bermejo No 195
Col. Palo de Santa Rita
La Paz, Baja
California Sur, México 23090
Phone: +52-612-1238430
Fax: +52-612-1253625
E-mail: amuhlia04@cibnor.mx

Michael C. Murrell
U.S. Environmental Protection Agency
Gulf Ecology Division
1 Sabine Island Drive
Gulf Breeze, FL 32561
Phone: 850-934-2433
E-mail: murrell.michael@epa.gov

Raymond G. Najjar
The Pennsylvania State University
Department of Meteorology
503 Walker Building
University Park, PA 16802-5013
Phone: 814-863-1586
E-mail: najjar@meteo.psu.edu

Karen M. Orcutt
University of Southern Mississippi
Department of Marine Science
1020 Balch Blvd.
Stennis Space Center, MS 39529
Phone: 228-688-3154
Fax: 228-688-1121
E-mail: karen.orcutt@usm.edu

Philip M. Orton
Lamont-Doherty Earth Observatory
61 Route 9W
Palisades, NY 10964
Phone: 845 365-8317
E-mail: orton@ldeo.columbia.edu

Christopher Osburn
Naval Research Laboratory Code 6114
4555 Overlook Ave. SW
Washington, DC 20375
Phone: 703-899-4828
E-mail: christopher.osburn@nrl.navy.mil

John H. Paul
University of South Florida
140 7th Ave. South
St Petersburg, FL 33701
Phone: 727-553-1168
E-mail: jpaul@marine.usf.edu

Tsung-Hung Peng
NOAA/AOML
4301 Rickenbacker Causeway
Miami, FL 33149
Phone: 305-361-4399
E-mail: tsung-hung.peng@noaa.gov

Charles H. Perry
USDA Forest Service
Northern Research Station
1992 Folwell Ave.
St. Paul, MN 55108
Phone: 651-649-5191
Fax: 651-649-5140
E-mail: charleshperry@fs.fed.us

Rodney T. Powell
LUMCON
8124 Highway 56
Chauvin, LA 70344
Phone: 985-851-2825
Fax: 985-851-2874
E-mail: rpowell@lumcon.edu

Ellen Raabe
U.S. Geological Survey
600 4th St. South
St. Petersburg, FL 33701
Phone: 727-803-8747 x3039
E-mail: eraabe@usgs.gov

Peter Raymond
Yale University
21 Sachem St.
New Haven, CT 06511
Phone: 203-432-0817
E-mail: peter.raymond@yale.edu

Mary Jo Richardson
Texas A&M University
3146 TAMU
Department of Oceanography
College Station, TX 77843
Phone: 979-845-7966
E-mail: mrichardson@ocean.tamu.edu

Joseph E. Salisbury
University of New Hampshire
Ocean Processes Analysis Lab
142 Morse Hall
Durham, NH 03824
Phone: 603-862-0849
E-mail: joe.salisbury@unh.edu

Robert H. Stav
University of North Carolina - Greensboro
Eberhart 312
321 McIver St.
Greensboro, NC 27412
Phone: 336-334-4979
E-mail: stavnr@uncg.edu

Ajit Subramaniam
National Science Foundation
4201 Wilson Blvd.
Arlington, VA 22230
Phone: 703-292-7592
E-mail: asubrama@nsf.gov

Eric Sundquist
U.S. Geological Survey
384 Woods Hole Rd.
Woods Hole, MA 02543
Phone: 508-457-2397
E-mail: esundqui@usgs.gov

Kathy A. Tedesco
U.S. Geological Survey
600 4th St. South
St. Petersburg, FL 33701
Phone: 727-803-8747 x3121
E-mail: ktedesco@usgs.gov

Hanqin Tian
Auburn University
School of Forestry and Wildlife Sciences
602 Duncan Drive
Auburn, AL 36849
Phone: 334-844-1059
E-mail: tianhan@auburn.edu

R. Eugene Turner
Louisiana State University
Coastal Ecology Inst. SCE
Baton Rouge, LA 70803
Phone: 225-578-6454
Fax: 225-578-6326
E-mail: euturne@lsu.edu

Baris M. Uz
NOAA Climate Program Office
1315 East West Highway
Silver Spring, MD 20910
Phone: 301-724-1247
E-mail: baris.uz@noaa.gov

Zhaohui Wang
University of South Florida
College of Marine Science
140 7th Ave. South
St. Petersburg, FL 33701
Phone: 727-553-3922
E-mail: awang@marine.usf.edu

Rik Wanninkhof
NOAA/AOML
4301 Rickenbacker Causeway
Miami, FL 33149
Phone: 305-361-4379
E-mail: rik.wanninkhof@noaa.gov

Lucian Wielopolski
Brookhaven National Laboratory
Environmental Sciences Department
Bldg. 490D
Upton, NY 11973
Phone: 631-344-3656
E-mail: lwielo@bnl.gov

Jerry Wiggert
The University of Southern Mississippi
Department of Marine Sciences
1020 Balch Blvd.
Stennis Space Center, MS 39529
Phone: 228-688-3491
Fax: 228-688-1121
E-mail: jerry.wiggert@usm.edu

Andrew R. Zimmerman
University of Florida
Department of Geological Sciences
241 Williamson Hall
Gainesville, FL 32611
Phone: 352-392-0070
E-mail: azimmer@ufl.edu

References Cited

Allison, M., Bianchi, T.S., McKee, B.A., and Sampere, T.P., 2007, Carbon burial on the river-dominated continental shelves: Impact of historical changes in sediment loading adjacent to the Mississippi River: Journal of Geophysical Resarch, v. 34, p. 1-6.

Álvarez-Góngora, C., and Herrera-Silveira, J.A., 2006, Variations of phytoplankton community structure related to water quality trends in a tropical karstic coastal zone: Marine Pollution Bulletin, v. 52, no. 1, p. 48-60.

Arcos-Espinosa, G., Medina-Santamaría, R., Méndez-Incera, F.J., and Jiménez-Hernández, S.B., 2008, Study of the salt wedge of the Panuco River, Mexico: Ingenieria Hidraulica en Mexico, v. 23, no. 3, p. 77-88.

Armstrong, R.A., Lee, C., Hedges, J.I., Honjo, S., and Wakeham, S.G., 2001, A new, mechanistic model for organic carbon fluxes in the ocean based on the quantitative association of POC with ballast minerals: Deep-Sea Research Part II, v. 49, no. 1-3, p. 219-236.

Arrigo, K., 2005, Marine microorganisms and global nutrient cycles: Nature, v. 437, no. 15, p. 349-355.

Avila, L.A., 2008, Highlights of the 2007 Atlantic and eastern North Pacific hurricane seasons -- A year of extremes in the Atlantic basin, AMS 28th Conference on Hurricanes and Tropical Meteorology: Miami, FL, American Meteorological Society, p. 3B.1-4. *http://ams.confex.com/ams/pdfpapers/137377.pdf*

Azetsu-Scott, K., and Passow, U., 2004, Ascending marine particles: Significance of transparent exopolymer particles (TEP) in the upper ocean: Limnology and Oceanography, v. 49, no. 3, p. 741-748

Baldocchi, D., 2008, 'Breathing' of the terrestrial biosphere: Lessons learned from a global network of carbon dioxide flux measurement systems: Australian Journal of Botany, v. 56, no. 1, p. 1-26.

Baschek, B., Farmer, D.M., and Garrett, C., 2006, Tidal fronts and their role in air-sea gas exchange: Journal of Marine Research, v. 64, no. 4, p. 483-515.

Beeman, P., 2008, Floods may yield record Gulf 'dead zone', Des Moines Register: Des Moines. *http://www.desmoinesregister.com/apps/pbcs.dll/article?AID=/20080626/NEWS/806260395*

Benke, A.C., and Cushing, C.E., 2005, Rivers of North America: Amsterdam, Academic Press, 1144 p.

Benway, H.M., and Doney, S.C., 2007, Advancing the integration of marine ecosystem dynamics and biogeochemistry: Second Annual Ocean Carbon and Biogeochemistry Summer Workshop: Eos, Transactions, v. 88, no. 47, doi: 10.1029/2007EO470007.

Bianchi, T.S., Filley, T., Dria, K., and Hatcher, P., 2004, Temporal variability in sources of dissolved organic carbon in the lower Mississippi River: Geochimica et Cosmochimica Acta, v. 68, p. 959-967.

Bianchi, T.S., Galler, J., and Allison, M.A., 2007, Hydrodynamic sorting and transport of terrestrially derived organic carbon in sediments of the Mississippi and Atchafalaya Rivers: Estuarine, Coastal and Shelf Science, v. 73, p. 211-222.

Bianchi, T.S., Lambert, C.D., Santschi, P.H., and Guo, L., 1997, Sources and transport of land-derived particulate and dissolved organic matter in the Gulf of Mexico (Texas shelf/slope): The use of lignin-phenols and loliolides as biomarkers: Organic Geochemistry, v. 27, p. 65-78.

Bianchi, T.S., Mitra, S., and McKee, M., 2002, Sources of terrestrially-derived carbon in the Lower Mississippi River and Louisiana shelf: Implications for differential sedimentation and transport at the coastal margin: Marine Chemistry, v. 77, no. 211-223.

Boehme, S.E., Sabine, C.L., and Reimers, C.E., 1998, CO_2 fluxes from a coastal transect: A time-series approach: Marine Chemistry, v. 63, no. 1-2, p. 49-67.

Boesch, D.F., 1999, The role of the Mississippi River in Gulf of Mexico hypoxia: Oversimplifications and confusion: Document submitted to the Gulf of Mexico Hypoxia Working Group, National Oceanic and Atmospheric Administration, 18 p.

Boesch, D.F., 2003, Continental shelf hypoxia: Some compelling answers: Gulf of Mexico Science, v. 21, p. 143-145.

Boning, C., 2008, Florida's rivers: Sarasota, Pineapple Press, 240 p.

Bortone, S.A., 2006, Recommendations on establishing a research strategy in the Gulf of Mexico to assess the effects of hurricanes on coastal ecosystems: Estuaries and Coasts, v. 29, no. 6, p. 1062-1066.

Boyer, E., 2008, Modeling watershed nutrient fluxes [presentation], *in* Ocean Carbon and Biogeochemistry Scoping Workshop on Terrestrial and Coastal Carbon Fluxes in the Gulf of Mexico, St. Petersburg, FL, May 6-8, 2008. Accessed at *http://www.whoi.edu/cms/files/boyer_ocb_large_36743.pdf*

Brown, A.V., Brown, K.B., Jackson, D.C., and Pierson, W.K., eds., 2005, Lower Mississippi River and its tributaries, *in* Benke, A.C., and Cushing, C.E., eds., Rivers of North America: Amsterdam, Academic Press, p. 231-281.

Burnett, W.C., Cowart, J.B., and Deetae, S., 1990, Radium in the Suwannee River and Estuary: Spring and river input to the Gulf of Mexico: Biogeochemistry, v. 10, no. 3, p. 237-255.

Cable, J.E., Burnett, W.C., Chanton, J.P., and Weatherly, G.L., 1996, Estimating groundwater discharge into the northeastern Gulf of Mexico using radon-222: Earth and Planetary Science Letters, v. 144, p. 591-604.

Cai, W.-J., 2003, Riverine inorganic carbon flux and rate of biological uptake in the Mississippi River plume: Geophysical Research Letters, v. 30, no. 2, 1032, doi:10.1029/2002GL016312.

Cai, W.-J., and Lohrenz, S.E., in press, Carbon, nitrogen, and phosphorus fluxes from the Mississippi River and the transformation and fate of biological elements in the river plume and the adjacent margin, *in* Liu, K.K., Atkinson, L., Quinones, R., and Talaue-McManus, L., eds., Carbon and nutrient fluxes in continental margins: a global synthesis: New York, Springer-Verlag.

Cai, W.-J., Gao, X., Chen, F., Huang, W.-J., Wang, Y., and Lohrenz, S.E., 2008, The dynamics of CO_2 in the Mississippi River plume and Northern Gulf of Mexico [presentation], *in* Ocean Carbon and Biogeochemistry Scoping Workshop on Terrestrial and Coastal Carbon Fluxes in the Gulf of Mexico, St. Petersburg, FL, May 6-8, 2008. Accessed at *http://www.whoi.edu/sbl/liteSite.do?litesiteid=23613*

Cai, W.-J., Wang, Y., Krest, J., and Moore, W.S., 2003, The geochemistry of dissolved inorganic carbon in a surficial groundwater aquifer in North Inlet, South Carolina, and the carbon fluxes to the coastal ocean: Geochimica et Cosmochimica Acta, v. 67, no. 4, p. 631-639.

Chavez, F.P., Takahashi, T., Cai, W.J., Friederich, G., Hales, B., Wanninkhof, R., and Feely, R.A., 2007, Coastal oceans, *in* King, A.W., Dilling, L., Zimmerman, G.P., Fairman, D.M., Houghton, R.A., Marland, G., Rose, A.Z., and Wilbanks, T.J., eds., The First State of the Carbon Cycle Report (SOCCR): The North American Carbon Budget and Implications for the Global Carbon Cycle: Asheville, NC, USA, National Oceanic and Atmospheric Administration, National Climatic Data Center, p. 156-166.

Chen, N., Bianchi, T.S., McKee, B.A., and Bland, J.M., 2001, Historical trends of hypoxia on the Louisiana shelf: Application of pigments as biomarkers: Organic Geochemistry, v. 32, p. 543-562.

Childers, D.S., Davis, S., Twilley, R., and Rivera-Monroy, V., 1998, Estuary-watershed coupling around the Gulf of Mexico, *in* Bianchi, T., Pennock, J., and Twilley, R., eds., Biogeochemistry of Gulf of Mexico estuaries: New York, Wiley, p. 211-235.

Corbett, D.R., Dillon, K., Burnett, W., and Chanton, J., 2000, Estimating the groundwater contribution into Florida Bay via natural tracers ^{222}Rn and CH_4: Limnology and Oceanography, v. 45, no. 7, p. 1546-1557.

Dagg, M., Benner, R., Lohrenz, S., and Lawrence, D., 2004, Transformation of dissolved and particulate materials on continental shelves influenced by large rivers: Plume processes: Continental Shelf Research, v. 24, no. 7-8, p. 833-858.

Dagg, M., Green, E., McKee, B., and Ortner, P., 1996, Biological removal of fine-grained lithogenic particles from a large river plume: Journal of Marine Research, v. 54, no. 1, p. 149-160.

Dagg, M.J., Ammerman, J.W., Amon, R.M.W., Gardner, W.S., Green, R.E., and Lohrenz, S.E., 2007, A review of water column processes influencing hypoxia in the northern Gulf of Mexico: Estuaries and Coasts, v. 30, p. 735-752.

Dagg, M.J., Bianchi, T., McKee, B., and Powell, R., 2008, Fates of dissolved and particulate materials from the Mississippi River immediately after discharge into the northern Gulf of Mexico, USA, during a period of low wind stress: Continental Shelf Research, v. 28, no. 12, p. 1443-1450.

Dahm, C., Edwards, R., and Gelwick, F., 2005, Gulf Coast rivers of the southwestern United States, *in* Benke, A.C., and Cushing, C.E., eds., Rivers of North America: Amsterdam, Academic Press.

Darrow, B.P., Walsh, J.J., Vargo, G.A., Masserini, R.T., Fanning, K.A., and Zhang, J.Z., 2003, A simulation study of the growth of benthic microalgae following the decline of a surface phytoplankton bloom: Continental Shelf Research, v. 23, no. 14-15, p. 1265-1283.

DeGrandpre, M.D., Olbu, G.J., Beatty, C.M., and Hammar, T.R., 2002, Air-sea CO_2 fluxes on the US Middle Atlantic Bight: Deep-Sea Research Part II, v. 49, no. 20, p. 4355-4367.

Del Castillo, C., Gilbes, F., Coble, P.G., and Muller-Karger, F.E., 2000, On the dispersal of riverine colored dissolved organic matter over the West Florida Shelf: Limnology and Oceanography, v. 45, no. 6, p. 1425-1432.

DeLong, M., 2005, Upper Mississippi River basin, *in* Benke, A.C., and Cushing, C.E., eds., Rivers of North America: Amsterdam, Academic Press, p. 327-374.

Denman, K., and Peña, M., 1999, A coupled 1-D biological/physical model of the northeast subarctic Pacific Ocean with iron limitation: Deep-Sea Research Part II, v. 46, no. 11-12, p. 2877-2908.

Dittmar, T., 2007, Non-riverine pathways of terrigenous carbon to the ocean, Eos, Transactions, v. 88, no. 52, abstract #B13G-08.

Doney, S.C., and Glover, D.M., 2005, Recent advances in the ocean carbon system: Eos, Transactions, v. 86, p. 399-400.

Doney, S.C., and Hood, M., 2002, A global ocean carbon observation system, a background report: UNESCO Intergovernmental Oceanographic Commission IOC/INF-1173, Global Ocean Observing System Report No. 118, 55 p.

Donner, S.D., and Kucharik, C.J., 2008, Corn-based ethanol production compromises goal of reducing nitrogen export by the Mississippi River: Proceedings of the National Academy of Sciences, v. 105, no. 11, p. 4513-4518.

Douglas, B.C., 2005, Gulf of Mexico and Atlantic coast sea level change: Geophysical Monograph, v. 161, p. 111-121.

Escobar-Briones, E.G., and Soto, L.A., 1997, Continental shelf benthic biomass in the western Gulf of Mexico: Continental Shelf Research, v. 17, no. 6, p. 585-604.

Fabry, V., Seibel, B., Feely, R., and Orr, J., 2008, Impacts of ocean acidification on marine fauna and ecosystem processes: ICES Journal of Marine Science, v. 65, no. 3, p. 414-432.

Fennel, K., Wilkin, J., Levin, J., Moisan, J., O'Reilly, J., and Haidvogel, D., 2006, Nitrogen cycling in the Middle Atlantic Bight: Results from a three-dimensional model and implications for the North Atlantic nitrogen budget: Global Biogeochemical Cycles, v. 20, no. 3, doi:10.1029/2005GB002456.

Flick, R.E., Murray, J.F., and Ewing, L.C., 2003, Trends in United States tidal datum statistics and tide range: Journal of Waterway, Port, Coastal and Ocean Engineering, v. 129, no. 4, p. 155-164.

Frankignoulle, M., and Borges, A.V., 2001, European continental shelf as a significant sink for atmospheric carbon dioxide: Global Biogeochemical Cycles, v. 15, no. 3, p. 569-576.

Frew, N.M., Goldman, J.C., Dennett, M.R., and Johnson, A.S., 1990, Impact of phytoplankton-generated surfactants on air-sea gas exchange: Journal of Geophysical Research, v. 95, no. C3, p. 3337-3352.

Gagliano, S.M., Meyer-Arendt, K.J., and Wicker, K.M., 1981, Land loss in the Mississippi River deltaic plain: Transactions of Gulf Coast Association of Geological Societies, v. 31, p. 295-300.

Galler, J.J., Bianchi, T.S., Allison, M.A., Campanella, R., and Wysocki, L.A., 2003, Biogeochemical implications of levee confinement in the lowermost Mississippi River: Eos, Transactions, v. 84, no. 44, p. 475-476.

Gardner, W.S., Cotner, J.B., Eadie, B.J., Cavaletto, J.F., Benner, R., and Chin-Leo, G., 1994, Mineralization of organic material and bacterial dynamics in Mississippi River plume water: Estuaries and Coasts, v. 17, no. 4, p. 816-828.

Goñi, M.A., Ruttenberg, K.C., and Eglinton, T.I., 1997, Sources and contribution of terrigenous organic carbon to surface sediments in the Gulf of Mexico: Nature, v. 389, no. 6648, p. 275-278.

Goñi, M.A., Ruttenberg, K.C., and Eglinton, T.I., 1998, A reassessment of the sources and importance of land-derived organic matter in surface sediments from the Gulf of Mexico: Geochimica et Cosmochimica Acta, v. 62, p. 3055-3075.

Gordon, E.S., and Goñi, M.A., 2003, Sources and distribution of terrigenous organic matter delivered by the Atchafalaya River to sediments in the northern Gulf of Mexico: Geochimica et Cosmochimica Acta, v. 67, p. 2359-2375.

Gower, J., Hu, C., Borstad, G., and King, S., 2006, Ocean color satellites show extensive lines of floating *Sargassum* in the Gulf of Mexico: IEEE Transactions on Geoscience and Remote Sensing, v. 44, no. 12, p. 3619-3625.

Gower, J., and King, S., 2008, Satellite images show the movement of floating *Sargassum* in the Gulf of Mexico and Atlantic Ocean: Nature Proceedings, v. 1894.1, no. 15. *http://precedings.nature.com/documents/1894/version/1/html*

Hales, B., Cai, W.-J., Mitchell, G., Sabine, C., and Schofield, O., 2008, North American continental margins: A synthesis and planning workshop: U.S. Carbon Cycle Science Program, 110 p.

Hallock, P., 2005, Global change and modern coral reefs: New opportunities to understand shallow-water carbonate depositional processes: Sedimentary Geology, v. 175, no. 1-4, p. 19-33.

He, R., 2008, Physical oceanography and circulation of the Gulf of Mexico [presentation], *in* Ocean Carbon and Biogeochemistry Scoping Workshop on Terrestrial and Coastal Carbon Fluxes in the Gulf of Mexico, St. Petersburg, FL, May 6-8, 2008.

He, R., and Weisberg, R.H., 2003, A Loop Current intrusion case study on the West Florida Shelf: Journal of Physical Oceanography, v. 33, no. 2, p. 465-477.

Hedges, J.I., and Parker, P.L., 1976, Land-derived organic matter in surface sediments from the Gulf of Mexico: Geochimica et Cosmochimica Acta, v. 40, no. 9, p. 1019-1029.

Hernández-Arana, H.A., Rowden, A.A., Attrill, M.J., Warwick, R.M., and Gold-Bouchot, G., 2003, Large-scale environmental influences on the benthic macroinfauna of the southern Gulf of Mexico: Estuarine, Coastal and Shelf Science, v. 58, no. 4, p. 825-841.

Hoegh-Guldberg, O., Mumby, P.J., Hooten, A.J., Steneck, R.S., Greenfield, P., Gomez, E., Harvell, C.D., Sale, P.F., Edwards, A.J., and Caldeira, K., 2007, Coral reefs under rapid climate change and ocean acidification: Science, v. 318, no. 5857, p. 1737-1742.

Hofmann, E., and Mannino, A., 2007, Integrated study of the carbon budget of the continental shelf of the Mid-Atlantic and South Atlantic Bights: Geophysical Research Abstracts, v. 9. http://www.cosis.net/abstracts/EGU2007/04439/EGU2007-J-04439.pdf

Hu, C., Muller-Karger, F.E., and Swarzenski, P.W., 2006, Hurricanes, submarine groundwater discharge, and Florida's red tides: Geophysical Research Letters, v. 33, L11601, doi:10.1029/2005GL025449.

Hudson, P., Hendrickson, D., Benke, A., Varela-Romero, A., Rodiles-Hernandez, R., and Minckley, W.L., 2005, Rivers of Mexico, in Benke, A.C., and Cushing, C.E., eds., Rivers of North America: Amsterdam, Academic Press, p. 1031-1084.

IOC, 1997, Workshop report on the transports and linkages of the Intra-Americas Sea (IAS): Intergovernmental Oceanographic Commission Workshop Report No. 162, 58 p. http://unesdoc.unesco.org/images/0012/001283/128357e.pdf

IPCC, 2007, Climate change 2007: Mitigation: Contribution of Working Group III to the Fourth Assessment Report of the Intergovernmental Panel on Climate Change: Cambridge, Cambridge University Press, 841 p.

Jahnke, R.A., in press, A global synthesis, in Liu, K.K., Atkinson, L., Quinones, R., and Talaue-McManus, L., eds., Carbon and nutrient fluxes in continental margins: A global synthesis: New York, Springer-Verlag.

Kaiser, M.J., and Pulsipher, A.G., 2007, The impact of weather and ocean forecasting on hydrocarbon production and pollution management in the Gulf of Mexico: Energy Policy, v. 35, no. 2, p. 966-983.

Keller, M., Schimel, D.S., Hargrove, W.W., and Hoffman, F.M., 2008, A continental strategy for the National Ecological Observatory Network: Frontiers in Ecology and the Environment, v. 6, no. 5, p. 282-284.

Kempe, S., and Pegler, K., 1991, Sinks and sources of CO_2 in coastal seas: The North Sea: Tellus B. v. 43, no. 2, p. 224-235.

Kennish, M.J., 2002, Environmental threats and environmental future of estuaries: Environmental Conservation, v. 29, no. 1, p. 78-107.

Kildow, J., 2006, Phase I. Florida's ocean and coastal economies report: National Ocean Economics Program, Florida Oceans and Coastal Council, 117 p. http://www.floridaoceanscouncil.org/meetings/files/Florida_Ocean_&_Coastal_Eco.pdf

Kildow, J., 2008, Phase II. Florida's ocean and coastal economies report: National Ocean Economics Program, Florida Oceans and Coastal Council, 205 p. http://www.floridaoceanscouncil.org/meetings/files/2008/06-17/Florida_Phase_II_Report_2008.pdf

King, A.W., Dilling, L., Zimmerman, G.P., Fairman, D.M., Houghton, R.A., Marland, G., Rose, A.Z., and Wilbanks, T.J., eds., 2007, The first state of the carbon cycle report (SOCCR): The North American carbon budget and implications for the global carbon cycle: National Oceanic and Atmospheric Administration, National Climatic Data Center, 242 p.

Kishi, M.J., Kashiwai, M., Ware, D.M., Megrey, B.A., Eslinger, D.L., Werner, F.E., Noguchi-Aita, M., Azumaya, T., Fujii, M., Hashimoto, S., Huang, D., Iizumi, H., Ishida, Y., Kang, S., Kantakov, G.A., Kim, H.-C., Komatsu, K., Navrotsky, V.V., Smith, S.L., Tadokoro, K., Tsuda, A., Yamamura, O., Yamanaka, Y., Yokouchi, K., Yoshie, N., Zhang, J., Zuenko, Y.I., and Zvalinsky, V.I., 2007, NEMURO--a lower trophic level model for the North Pacific marine ecosystem: Ecological Modelling, v. 202, no. 1-2, p. 12-25.

Kleypas, J.A., Feely, R.A., Fabry, V.J., Langdon, C., Sabine, C.L., and Robbins, L.L., 2006, Impacts of ocean acidification on coral reefs and other marine calcifiers: A guide for future research: A report of a workshop held 18-20 April 2005, St. Petersburg, FL, sponsored by NSF, NOAA, and the U.S. Geological Survey, 88 p.

Ko, D.S., Preller, R.H., and Martin, P.J., 2003, An experimental real-time Intra-Americas Sea ocean nowcast/forecast system for coastal prediction, in 32nd Conference on Broadcast Meteorology/31st Conference on Radar Meteorology/Fifth Conference on Coastal Atmospheric and Oceanic Prediction and Processes, Seattle, WA, p. 5.2, http://ams.confex.com/ams/pdfpapers/64664.pdf

Kortzinger, A., 2003, A significant CO_2 sink in the tropical Atlantic Ocean associated with the Amazon River plume: Geophysical Research Letters, v. 30, no. 24, doi:10.1029/2003GL018841.

Krest, J.M., Moore, W.S., and Rama, 1999, ^{226}Ra and ^{228}Ra in the mixing zones of the Mississippi and Atchafalaya Rivers: Indicators of groundwater input: Marine Chemistry v. 64, p. 129-152.

Kvenvolden, K.A., and Lorenson, T.D., 2007, A global inventory of natural gas hydrate occurrence: U.S. Geological Survey. *http://walrus.wr.usgs.gov/globalhydrate/poster.pdf*

Lee, C., Wakeham, S., and Arnosti, C., 2004, Particulate organic matter in the sea: The composition conundrum: AMBIO: A Journal of the Human Environment, v. 33, no. 8, p. 565-575.

Lefèvre, N., Aiken, J., Rutllant, J., Daneri, G., Lavender, S., and Smyth, T., 2002, Observations of pCO$_2$ in the coastal upwelling off Chile: Spatial and temporal extrapolation using satellite data: Journal of Geophysical Research-Oceans, v. 107, no. C6, p. 8.1-8.15.

Lenes, J., Darrow, B., Walsh, J., Prospero, J., He, R., Weisberg, R., Vargo, G., and Heil, C., 2008, Saharan dust and phosphatic fidelity: A three-dimensional biogeochemical model of *Trichodesmium* as a nutrient source for red tides on the West Florida Shelf: Continental Shelf Research, v. 28, no. 9, p. 1091-1115.

Lenes, J.M., Darrow, B.P., Cattrall, C., Heil, C.A., Callahan, M., Vargo, G.A., Byrne, R.H., Prospero, J.M., Bates, D.E., Fanning, K.A., and Walsh, J.J., 2001, Iron fertilization and the *Trichodesmium* response on the West Florida Shelf: Limnology and Oceanography, v. 46, no. 6, p. 1261-1277.

Liu, K.K., Iseki, K., and Chao, S.Y., 2000, Continental margin carbon fluxes, *in* Hanson, R.B., Field, J.G., and Ducklow, H.W., eds., The changing ocean carbon cycle: A midterm synthesis of the Joint Global Ocean Flux Study: Cambridge, Cambridge University Press, p. 187-239.

Lohrenz, S.E., 2008, Gulf of Mexico carbon cycling [presentation], *in* Ocean Carbon and Biogeochemistry Scoping Workshop on Terrestrial and Coastal Carbon Fluxes in the Gulf of Mexico, St. Petersburg, FL, May 6-8, 2008.

Lohrenz, S.E., and Cai, W.-J., 2006, Satellite ocean color assessment of air-sea fluxes of CO$_2$ in a river-dominated coastal margin: Geophysical Research Letters, v. 33, no. 1, doi:10.1029/2005GL023942.

Lohrenz, S.E., and Cai, W.-J., 2008, North America's Gulf of Mexico coast: North American continental margins report.

Lohrenz, S.E., Fahnenstiel, G.L., Redalje, D.G., Lang, G.A., Chen, X., Dagg, M.J., 1997, Variations in primary production of northern Gulf of Mexico continental shelf waters linked to nutrient inputs from the Mississippi River: Marine Ecology Progress Series, v. 155, p. 45-54.

López-Méndez, V., Zavala-Hidalgo, J., and Romero-Centeno, R., 2008, Analysis of the extreme flooding during October 2007 in Tabasco, Mexico using the WRF model: 9th Annual WRF (Weather Research & Forecasting Model) Users' Workshop: Boulder, CO, 23-27 June 2008, National Center for Atmospheric Research.

Lueker, T.J., Walker, S.J., Vollmer, M.K., Keeling, R.F., Nevison, C.D., and Weiss, R.F., 2003, Coastal upwelling air-sea fluxes revealed in atmospheric observations of O$_2$/N$_2$, CO$_2$ and N$_2$O: Geophysical Research Letters, v. 30, no. 6, 1292, doi:10.1029/2002GL016615.

Mackenzie, F.T., Lerman, A., and Ver, L.M.B., 1998, Role of the continental margin in the global carbon balance during the past three centuries: Geology, v. 26, no. 5, p. 423-426.

Maloney, E.D., and Hartmann, D.L., 2000, Modulation of hurricane activity in the Gulf of Mexico by the Madden-Julian Oscillation: Science, v. 287, no. 5460, p. 2002-2004.

Marmorino, G.O., and Trump, C.L., 1996, High-resolution measurements made across a tidal intrusion front: Journal of Geophysical Research, v. 101, p. 25661-25674.

McGillis, W.R., Edson, J.B., Hare, J.E., and Fairall, C.W., 2001a, Direct covariance air-sea CO$_2$ fluxes: Journal of Geophysical Research, v. 106, no. C8, p. 16729-16746.

McGillis, W.R., Edson, J.B., Ware, J.D., Dacey, J.W.H., Hare, J.E., Fairall, C.W., and Wanninkhof, R., 2001b, Carbon dioxide flux techniques performed during GasEx-98: Marine Chemistry, v. 75, no. 4, p. 267-280.

McKee, B., 2003, RIOMar: The transport, transformation, and fate of carbon in river-dominated ocean margins: A report of the RioMAR community workshop, Tulane University, 8 p.

McKee, B.A., Aller, R.C., Allison, M.A., Bianchi, T.S., and Kineke, G.C., 2004, Transport and transformation of dissolved and particulate materials on continental margins influenced by major rivers: Benthic boundary layer and seabed processes: Continental Shelf Research, v. 24, p. 899-926.

McKee, B.A., and Baskaran, M., 1999, Sedimentary processes of Gulf of Mexico estuaries, *in* Bianchi, T., Pennock, J., and Twilley, R., eds., Biogeochemistry of Gulf of Mexico estuaries: New York, Wiley, p. 63-85.

Merino, M., 1997, Upwelling on the Yucatan Shelf: Hydrographic evidence: Journal of Marine Systems, v. 13, no. 1-4, p. 101-121.

Milkov, A.V., and Sassen, R., 2000, Thickness of the gas hydrate stability zone, Gulf of Mexico continental slope: Marine and Petroleum Geology, v. 17, no. 9, p. 981-991.

Mitsch, W.J., Day, J.W., Jr., Gilliam, J.W., Groffman, P.M., Hey, D.L., Randall, G.W., and Wang, N., 2001, Reducing nitrogen loading to the Gulf of Mexico from the Mississippi River Basin: Strategies to counter a persistent ecological problem: BioScience, v. 51, no. 5, p. 373-388.

Monahan, E.C., and Spillane, M.C., 1984, The role of oceanic whitecaps in air-sea gas exchange, *in* Brutsaert, W., and Jirka, G.H., eds., Gas transfer at water surfaces: Hingham, MA, D. Reidal, p. 495-503.

Morel, F., and Hering, J., 1993, Principles and applications of aquatic chemistry: New York, Wiley, 588 p.

Morse, J.W., Andersson, A.J., and Mackenzie, F.T., 2006, Initial responses of carbonate-rich shelf sediments to rising atmospheric pCO_2 and "ocean acidification": Role of high Mg-calcites: Geochimica et Cosmochimica Acta, v. 70, no. 23, p. 5814-5830.

Muhlia Melo, A., 2008, Programa Mexicano del C (PMC): Mexican Carbon Program [presentation], *in* Ocean Carbon and Biogeochemistry Scoping Workshop on Terrestrial and Coastal Carbon Fluxes in the Gulf of Mexico, St. Petersburg, FL, May 6-8, 2008.

Najjar, R., 2008, Eastern U.S. continental shelf carbon budget: Modeling data assimilation and analysis [presentation], *in* Ocean Carbon and Biogeochemistry Scoping Workshop on Terrestrial and Coastal Carbon Fluxes in the Gulf of Mexico, St. Petersburg, FL, May 6-8, 2008.

Nipper, M., Chavez, J.A.S., and Tunnell, J.W., Jr., 2004, Gulfbase: Resource database for Gulf of Mexico research: Corpus Christi, Texas A&M University. *http://www.gulfbase.org*

NOAA, 2007, Gulf of Mexico ecosystems & hypoxia assessment (NGOMEX): Silver Spring, National Oceanic and Atmospheric Administration, National Ocean Service, National Centers for Coastal Ocean Science, Center for Sponsored Coastal Ocean Research. *http://www.cop.noaa.gov/stressors/pollution/current/gomex-factsheet.html*

NOAA, 2008, Regional mean sea level trends: Silver Spring, MD, National Oceanic and Atmospheric Administration. *http://tidesandcurrents.noaa.gov/sltrends/slrmap.html*

NRC, 2002, Florida Bay research programs and their relation to the Comprehensive Everglades Restoration Plan: Washington, DC, National Academies Press, 54 p.

NRC, 2007, Earth science and applications from space: National imperatives for the next decade and beyond: Washington, DC, National Academies Press, 456 p.

Oey, L.Y., Ezer, T., and Lee, H.-C., 2005, Loop Current, rings and related circulation in the Gulf of Mexico: A review of numerical models and future challenges, *in* Sturges, W., and Lugo-Fernandez, A., eds., Circulation in the Gulf of Mexico: Observations and models; Geophysical Monograph Series v. 161: Washington, DC, American Geophysical Union, p. 11-29.

Ogle, S., and Davis, K., 2006, Science plan: Mid-continent intensive campaign of the North American Carbon Program: North American Carbon Program, 11 p. *http://www.nacarbon.org/nacp/documents/NACP_MCI_SciPlan_8-06.pdf*

Onstad, G.D., Canfield, D.E., Quay, P.D., and Hedges, J.I., 2000, Sources of particulate organic matter in rivers from the continental USA: Lignin phenol and stable carbon isotope compositions: Geochimica et Cosmochimica Acta, v. 64, p. 3539-3546.

Orr, J.C., Fabry, V.J., Aumont, O., Bopp, L., Doney, S.C., Feely, R.A., Gnanadesikan, A., Gruber, N., Ishida, A., Joos, F., Key, R.M., Lindsay, K., Maier-Reimer, E., Matear, R., Monfray, P., Mouchet, A., Najjar, R.G., Plattner, G.-K., Rodgers, K.B., Sabine, C.L., Sarmiento, J.L., Schlitzer, R., Slater, R.D., Totterdell, I.J., Weirig, M.-F., Yamanaka, Y., and Yool, A., 2005, Anthropogenic ocean acidification over the twenty-first century and its impact on calcifying organisms: Nature, v. 437, no. 7059, p. 681-686.

Parrish, D.D., Hahn, C.J., Williams, E.J., Norton, R.B., Fehsenfeld, F.C., Singh, H.B., Shetter, J.D., Gandrud, B.W., and Ridley, B.A., 1992, Indications of photochemical histories of Pacific air masses from measurements of atmospheric trace species at Point Arena, California: Journal of Geophysical Research, v. 97, no. D14, p. 15883-15901.

Peng, T.-H., and Langdon, C., 2007, Gulf of Mexico and East Coast Carbon Cruise (GOMECC): Cruise report: Silver Spring, MD, National Oceanic and Atmospheric Administration. *http://www.aoml.noaa.gov/ocd/gcc/GOMECC/CruiseReportfinal.pdf*

Pennock, J.R., Boyer, J.N., Herrera-Silveira, J.A., Iverson, R.L., Whitledge, T.E., Mortazavi, B., and Comin, F.A., 1999, Nutrient behavior and phytoplankton production in Gulf of Mexico estuaries, *in* Bianchi, T., Pennock, J., and Twilley, R., eds., Biogeochemistry of Gulf of Mexico estuaries: New York, Wiley, p. 109-162.

Port of Houston Authority, 2008, General information: Houston, Port of Houston Authority. *http://www.portofhouston.com/geninfo/overview1.html*

Rabalais, N.N., Turner, R.E., and Wiseman Jr, W.J., 2002, Hypoxia in the Gulf of Mexico, a k.a. "The Dead Zone": Annual Review of Ecology and Systematics, v. 33, p. 235-263.

Raymond, P., Oh, N., Turner, R., and Broussard, W., 2008, Anthropogenically enhanced fluxes of water and carbon from the Mississippi River: Nature, v. 451, no. 7177, p. 449-452.

Raymond, P.A., and Cole, J.J., 2003, Increase in the export of alkalinity from North America's largest river: Science, v. 301, no. 5629, p. 88-91.

Rutkowski, C.M., Burnett, W.C., Iverson, R.L., and Chanton, J.P., 1999, The effect of groundwater seepage on nutrient delivery and seagrass distribution in the northeastern Gulf of Mexico: Estuaries, v. 22, p. 1033-1040.

Sager, W., 2007, AUV and multibeam survey on the Florida Escarpment, 2007 Offshore Technology Conference, Houston, TX, 30 April - 3 May 2007. *http://www.otcnet. org/2007/technical/schedule/documents/otc184791.pdf*

Sánchez-Gil, P., Yáñez-Arancibia, A., Ramírez-Gordillo, J., Day, J.W., and Templet, P.H., 2004, Some socio-economic indicators in the Mexican states of the Gulf of Mexico: Ocean & Coastal Management, v. 47, no. 11-12, p. 581-596.

Santschi, P.H., Oktay, S.D., and Cifuentes, L., 2007, Carbon isotopes and iodine concentrations in a Mississippi River delta core recording land use, sediment transport, and dam building in the river's drainage basin: Marine Environmental Research, v. 63, no. 3, p. 278-290.

Sarmiento, J.L., and Wofsy, S.C., 1999, A U.S. carbon cycle science plan; Report of the Carbon and Climate Working Group for the U.S. Global Change Research Program: Washington, U.S. Global Change Research Program, 69 p.

Schifter, I., González-Macías, C., Miranda, A., and López-Salinas, E., 2005, Air emissions assessment from offshore oil activities in Sonda de Campeche, Mexico: Environmental Monitoring and Assessment, v. 109, no. 1, p. 135-145.

Schroeder, W.W., and Wiseman, W.J., 1999, Geology and hydrodynamics of Gulf of Mexico estuaries, *in* Bianchi, T., Pennock, J., and Twilley, R., eds., Biogeochemistry of Gulf of Mexico estuaries: New York, Wiley, p. 3-28.

SCOR and LOICZ, 2004, Submarine groundwater discharge: Management implications, measurements and effects: International Hydrological Program (IHP) and Intergovernmental Oceanographic Commission (IOC), IHP-VI series on groundwater no. 5; IOC manuals and guides no. 44, 35 p. *http://unesdoc.unesco.org/images/0013/001344/134436e. pdf*

Seitzinger, S.P., Harrison, J.A., Dumont, E., Beusen, A.H.W., and Bouwman, A.F., 2005, Sources and delivery of carbon, nitrogen, and phosphorus to the coastal zone: An overview of Global Nutrient Export from Watersheds (NEWS) models and their application: Global Biogeochemical Cycles v. 19, p. GB4S01.

Siemens, A.H., Moreno-Casasola, P., and Bueno, C.S., 2006, The metabolization of dunes and wetlands by the City of Veracruz, Mexico: Journal of Latin American Geography, v. 5, p. 7-29.

Smith, S.V., and Hollibaugh, J.T., 1993, Coastal metabolism and the oceanic organic carbon balance: Reviews of Geophysics, v. 31, no. 1, p. 75-89.

Smith, S.V., and Mackenzie, F.T., 1987, The ocean as a net heterotrophic system: Implications from the carbon biogeochemical cycle: Global Biogeochemical Cycles, v. 1, no. 3, p. 187-198.

Solis, R.S., and Powell, G.L., 1999, Hydrography, mixing characteristics, and residence times of Gulf of Mexico estuaries, *in* Bianchi, T., Pennock, J., and Twilley, R., eds., Biogeochemistry of Gulf of Mexico estuaries: New York, Wiley, p. 29-61.

Stokstad, E., 1999, Scarcity of rain, stream gages threatens forecasts: Science, v. 285, p. 1199-1200.

Stumpf, R.P., and Haines, J.W., 1998, Variations in tidal level in the Gulf of Mexico and implications for tidal wetlands: Estuarine, Coastal and Shelf Science, v. 46, p. 165-173.

Sundquist, E., 2008, From carbon footprint to carbon pathway: carbon-cycle science at a crossroads [presentation], *in* Ocean Carbon and Biogeochemistry Scoping Workshop on Terrestrial and Coastal Carbon Fluxes in the Gulf of Mexico, St. Petersburg, FL, May 6-8, 2008.

Sutyrin, G.G., Rowe, G.D., Rothstein, L.M., and Ginis, I., 2003, Baroclinic eddy interactions with continental slopes and shelves: Journal of Physical Oceanography, v. 33, no. 1, p. 283-291.

Ternon, J.F., Oudot, C., Dessier, A., and Diverres, D., 2000, A seasonal tropical sink for atmospheric CO_2 in the Atlantic Ocean: The role of the Amazon River discharge: Marine Chemistry, v. 68, no. 3, p. 183-201.

Thieler, E.R., and Hammar-Klose, E.S., 2000, National assessment of coastal vulnerability to future sea-level rise: Preliminary results for the US Gulf of Mexico coast: U.S. Geological Survey Open-File Report 00-179.

Thomas, H., Bozec, Y., Elkalay, K., and de Baar, H.J.W., 2004, Enhanced open ocean storage of CO_2 from shelf sea pumping: Science, v. 304, no. 5673, p. 1005-1008.

Tokoro, T., Watanabe, A., Kayanne, H., Nadaoka, K., Tamura, H., Nozak, K., Kato, K., and Negishi, A., 2007, Measurement of air-water CO_2 transfer at four coastal sites using a chamber method: Journal of Marine Systems, v. 66, no. 1-4, p. 140-149.

Trefry, J., Butterfield, D., Metz, S., Massoth, G., Trocine, R., and Feely, R., 1994, Trace metals in hydrothermal solutions from Cleft segment on the southern Juan de Fuca Ridge: Journal of Geophysical Research, v. 99, p. 4925-4936.

Tsunogai, S., Watanabe, S., and Sato, T., 1999, Is there a continental shelf pump for the absorption of atmospheric CO_2? Tellus B, v. 51, no. 3, p. 701-712.

Tunnell, J.W., Jr., 2007, Introduction, *in* Tunnell, John W., Jr., Chavez, E.A., and Withers, K., eds., Coral reefs of the Southern Gulf of Mexico: Corpus Christi, Texas A&M University Press, p. 1-4.

Turner, R., Rabalais, N., Alexander, R., McIsaac, G., and Howarth, R., 2007, Characterization of nutrient, organic carbon, and sediment loads and concentrations from the Mississippi River into the northern Gulf of Mexico: Estuaries and Coasts, v. 30, no. 5, p. 773-790.

Turner, R.E., and Rabalais, N.N., 1991, Changes in Mississippi River quality this century: BioScience, v. 41, no. 3, p. 140-147.

Turner, R.E., and Rabalais, N.N., 2004, Suspended sediment, C, N, P, and Si yields from the Mississippi River Basin: Hydrobiologia, v. 511, p. 79-89.

Turner, R.E., Rabalais, N.N., and Justic, D., 2008, Gulf of Mexico hypoxia: Alternate states and a legacy: Environmental Science and Technology, v. 42 no. 7, p. 2323-2327.

Turner, R.E., Rabalais, N.N., Swenson, E.M., Kasprzak, M., and Romaire, T., 2005, Summer hypoxia in the northern Gulf of Mexico and its prediction from 1978 to 1995: Marine Environmental Research, v. 59, no. 1, p. 65-77.

Upstill-Goddard, R., 2006, Air-sea gas exchange in the coastal zone: Estuarine, Coastal and Shelf Science, v. 70, no. 3, p. 388-404.

U.S. EPA, 1999, Ecological condition of estuaries in the Gulf of Mexico: U.S. Environmental Protection Agency Office of Research and Development, National Health and Environmental Effects Research Laboratory, Gulf Ecology Division EPA 620-R-98-004, 71 p. *http://www.epa.gov/ged/docs/EcoCondEstuariesGOM_print.pdf*

U.S. EPA, 2007, Hypoxia in the Northern Gulf of Mexico: An update by the EPA Science Advisory Board: U.S. Environmental Protection Agency EPA-SAB-08-003, 333 p.

Vlahos, P., Chen, R.F., and Repeta, D.J., 2002, Dissolved organic carbon in the Mid-Atlantic Bight: Deep-Sea Research Part II, v. 49, no. 20, p. 4369-4385.

Vukovich, F.M., 2007, Climatology of ocean features in the Gulf of Mexico using satellite remote sensing data: Journal of Physical Oceanography, v. 37, no. 3, p. 689-707.

Walker, N.D., Wiseman, W.J., Jr., Rouse, L.J., Jr., and Babin, A., 2005, Effects of river discharge, wind stress, and slope eddies on circulation and the satellite-observed structure of the Mississippi River plume: Journal of Coastal Research, v. 21, p. 1228-1244.

Walsh, J.J., 1991, Importance of continental margins in the marine biogeochemical cycling of carbon and nitrogen: Nature, v. 350, no. 6313, p. 53-55.

Walsh, J.J., Dieterle, D.A., Meyers, M.B., and Muller-Karger, F.E., 1989, Nitrogen exchange at the continental margin: a numerical study of the Gulf of Mexico: Progress in Oceanography, v. 23, p. 245-301.

Walsh, J.J., Weisberg, R.H., Dieterle, D.A., He, R., Darrow, B.P., Jolliff, J.K., Lester, K.M., Vargo, G.A., Kirkpatrick, G.J., Fanning, K.A., Sutton, T.T., Jochens, A.E., Biggs, D.C., Nababan, B., Hu, C., and Muller-Karger, F.E., 2003, Phytoplankton response to intrusions of slope water on the West Florida Shelf: Models and observations: Journal of Geophysical Research, v. 108, no. C6, 3190, doi:10.1029/2002JC001406.

Wang, S.L., Chen, C.T., Hong, G.H., and Chung, C.S., 2000, Carbon dioxide and related parameters in the East China Sea: Continental Shelf Research, v. 20, no. 4-5, p. 525-544.

Wang, X.C., Chen, R.F., and Gardner, G.B., 2004, Sources and transport of dissolved and particulate organic carbon in the Mississippi River estuary and adjacent coastal waters of the northern Gulf of Mexico: Marine Chemistry, v. 89, no. 1-4, p. 241-256.

Wanninkhof, R., 2008, CO_2 flux dynamics in the Gulf of Mexico [presentation], *in* Ocean Carbon and Biogeochemistry Scoping Workshop on Terrestrial and Coastal Carbon Fluxes in the Gulf of Mexico, St. Petersburg, FL, May 6-8, 2008.

Wanninkhof, R., Asher, W., and Monahan, E.C., eds., 1995, The influence of bubbles on air-water gas exchange results from gas transfer experiments during WABEX-93, *in* Air-water Gas Transfer: Selected papers from the Third Symposium on air-water gas transfer, Hanau, Germany, Aeow Verlag, p. 239-255.

Wanninkhof, R., Hitchcock, G., Wiseman, W.J., Vargo, G.A., Ortner, P.B., Asher, W., Ho, D.T., Schlosser, P., Dickson, M.-L., Masserini, R.T., Fanning, K.A., and Zhang, J.-Z., 1997, Gas exchange, dispersion, and biological productivity on the West Florida Shelf: Results from a Lagrangian tracer study: Geophysical Research Letters, v. 24, no. 14, p. 1767-1770.

Wanninkhof, R., and Knox, M., 1996, Chemical enhancement of CO_2 exchange in natural waters: Limnology and Oceanography, v. 41, no. 4, p. 689-697.

Wanninkhof, R., Lohrenz, S., and Cai, W.-J., 2007, Estimating air-sea carbon dioxide fluxes in the river-dominated northern Gulf of Mexico, *in* Northern Gulf Institute Conference, Biloxi, MS, May 16-17, 2007. *http://www.northerngulfinstitute.org/ngiconference/presentations/NGI_Conf_Presentations_2007/19-Wanninkhof_NOAA_Project.pdf*

Ward, M., Harris, P., and Ward, A., 2005, Gulf Coast rivers of the southeastern United States, *in* Benke, A.C., and Cushing, C.E., eds., Rivers of North America: Amsterdam, Academic Press, p. 125-180.

Waterson, E.J., and Canuel, E.A., 2008, Sources of sedimentary organic matter in the Mississippi River and adjacent Gulf of Mexico as revealed by lipid biomarker and δ^{13}C TOC analyses: Organic Geochemistry, v. 39, no. 4, p. 422-439.

Weisberg, R.H., Black, B., and Li, Z., 2000, An upwelling case study on Florida's west coast: Journal of Geophysical Research, v. 105(C5), p. 11,459-11,469.

Wysocki, L.A., Bianchi, T.S., Powell, R.T., and Reuss, N., 2006, Spatial variability in the coupling of organic carbon, nutrients, and phytoplankton pigments in surface waters and sediments of the Mississippi River plume: Estuarine, Coastal and Shelf Science, v. 69, no. 1-2, p. 47-63.

Yáñez-Arancibia, A., and Day, J.W., 2004a, The Gulf of Mexico: Towards an integration of coastal management with large marine ecosystem management: Ocean & Coastal Management, v. 47, no. 11-12, p. 537-563.

Yáñez-Arancibia, A., and Day, J.W., 2004b, Environmental sub-regions in the Gulf of Mexico coastal zone: The ecosystem approach as an integrated management tool: Ocean & Coastal Management, v. 47, no. 11-12, p. 727-757.

Yáñez-Arancibia, A., and Day, J.W., Jr., 2006, Hydrology, water budget, and residence time in the Terminos Lagoon Estuarine System, Southern Gulf of Mexico, *in* Coastal Hydrology and Processes: Proceedings of the American Institute of Hydrology 25th Anniversary Meeting & International Conference, Water Resources Publication, p. 423-436.

Yáñez-Arancibia, A., Lara-Domínguez, A.L., Rojas Galaviz, J.L., Zárate Lomeli, D.J., Villalobos Zapata, G.J., and Sánchez-Gil, P., 1999, Integrating science and management on coastal marine protected areas in the Southern Gulf of Mexico: Ocean & Coastal Management, v. 42, no. 2-4, p. 319-344.

Yuan, D., 2002, A numerical study of barotropicly forced intrusion in DeSoto Canyon: Journal of Geophysical Research, v. 107, no. C2, doi:10.1029/2001JC00079.

Zappa, C.J., Raymond, P.A., Terray, E.A., and McGillis, W.R., 2003, Variation in surface turbulence and the gas transfer velocity over a tidal cycle in a macro-tidal estuary: Estuaries and Coasts, v. 26, no. 6, p. 1401-1415.

Zavala-Hidalgo, J., Gallegos-García, A., Martínez-López, B., Morey, S.L., and O'Brien, J.J., 2006, Seasonal upwelling on the western and southern shelves of the Gulf of Mexico: Ocean Dynamics, v. 56, no. 3, p. 333-338.

Zektser, I.S., Dzhamalov, R., Everett, L.G., eds., 2007, Submarine groundwater: Boca Raton, CRC Press, 466 p.

Zhai, W., Dai, M., Cai, W.-J., Wang, Y., and Hong, H., 2005, The partial pressure of carbon dioxide and air-sea fluxes in the northern South China Sea in spring, summer and autumn: Marine Chemistry, v. 96, no. 1-2, p. 87-97.

Zhao, D., Toba, Y., Suzuki, Y., and Komori, S., 2003, Effect of wind waves on air-sea gas exchange: Proposal of an overall CO_2 transfer velocity formula as a function of breaking-wave parameter: Tellus B, v. 55, p. 478-487.

USGS

L.L. Robbins and others — Ocean Carbon and Biogeochemistry Scoping Workshop on Terrestrial and Coastal Carbon Fluxes in the Gulf of Mexico, St. Petersburg, FL, May 6-8, 2008 — OFR 2009-1070